THE 6 FIGURE PRISONER

UNLOCK YOUR MIND AND GET RICH REGARDLESS

MALIK IBN LEROW

The 6 Figure Prisoner
Unlock Your Mind And Get Rich Regardless

Big Player Publishing

ISBN 9780578375243(paperback)
ISBN 9798218039677(ebook)

CONTENTS

DEDICATION v

PROLOGUE 1

FOR STARTERS: 5

FIRST QUARTER

THE PRINCE OF DARKNESS 14

NEGRO WALLSTREET 17

RICHEST MAN EVER 21

HISTORY OF FOREX 27

SECOND QUARTER

THE ECONOMICS OF FOREX 32

TRADERS AND BROKERS 35

STOCKS VS FOREX 39

CRYPTO 43

THIRD QUARTER

METAVERSE 50
NFT 53
BLOCKCHAIN 57
SMART CONTRACTS 61
DEFI 63

FOURTH QUARTER

IGNORANCE OF THE LAW IS NO EXCUSE 72
CHAKRAS 79
POWER WITHIN 83
TOXIC SOCIAL MEDIA USAGE 87
PHYSICAL FITNESS 91
PLANT-BASED LIFESTYLE 95

OVERTIME

REPLACE YOUR PRISON WITH EIN 104
CREDIT IS KING 109
DIGITAL ENTREPRENEURSHIP 115
EPILOGUE 123
GLOSSARY OF TERMS 127
ABOUT AUTHOR 131

DEDICATION

I want to dedicate this book to my father because the apple fell right beside the tree, to my great grandmother who passed away shortly after I was convicted at trial, to the wrongfully convicted and over-sentenced, and lastly, to the ones who have been where I've been, done what I've done, and come from where I come from, but will never change because they're stuck in their ways.

PROLOGUE

"Neither slavery nor involuntary servitude, except as a punishment for crime, where the party shall have been duly convicted shall exist within the United States, or any place subject to the jurisdiction." This is the 13th Amendment to the U.S. Constitution and was passed by Congress on January 31 1865. It came into effect on December 6, 1865. The US has 5% of the world population, but 25% of the world's prisoners; the United States of America has the highest incarceration worldwide. One in 17 white males and one in three black males have a lifetime likelihood of imprisonment. What that means is, for every 17 white males, only one has a probability of going to prison in their life and one in three black males has a possibility or likelihood of going to prison. Black men are only 6.5% of the US population, but black men are 40.2% of the prison population. It's more blacks under supervision than slaves of the 1850's. Now, there's just something to think about. You can call it what you want, but it is what it is. Slavery was an economic system and so is the jail/prison system. The 13th Amendment was not intended for blacks or African Americans to be free; it was a means to take away the stigma in America due to slavery. All the while, they knew that the exception to the rule would justify them re-enslaving blacks under the guise of crime and punishment. Now, you will see a line from an increase in convictions or the enslavement of blacks down to current a society where the prison system has been more so monetized. And what I mean by "monetized" is, big corporations and politicians are invested in free labor of prisoners. For example, the American Legislative Exchange Council, or ALEC has an influence on laws through big companies and state legislators. In plain terms, big companies and state legislators meet up and discuss various wants and needs that certain bills - if passed into law - will serve them politically and serve companies financially.

A lot of things are put out there to increase crime, and due to increase in crime in some shape, form or fashion, the companies profit. For example, in the music industry, the rap music is a primary influence to young blacks. It glamorizes crime and paints it as the only way for young black males to get money. Also, it glamorizes violence and the likes. It's no coincidence that only certain types of music get mainstream play, and that's because it serves certain agenda. These big companies make sure that the music does get put out there, and then they make sure there's a turnover rate. So, if I'm invested in a company that puts the music that promote violence and crime, I can turn around and open up several private prisons for my financial gain. By showing a rapper flexing a whole bunch of money, fancy cars and all that, he can sing about selling drugs and then influence more of his kind to want to sell drugs, which in turn is going to lead to more crimes and violence. When you free a people, who have less knowledge than you, and have less resources than you, then you pretty much already know who's more likely to have to commit a crime out of necessity or survival. So, if the scale wasn't balanced out the gate, and people that don't have your best interest have a major influence over the mind of the youth, they can bank on slavery indefinitely, through evolution.

Now, what we have is a majority of crimes and wrong decisions being made out of ignorance, or out of habit. What we need to do now is, increase our knowledge, take advantage of our opportunities and change our habits for the better in order to break the cycle.

FOR STARTERS:

First off, I want to say, "Be like me, and you're going to prison. Learn from me, and you're going places." Don't be like me. This book is by no means glamorizing the prison lifestyle or encouraging you to go to prison in order to get six figures. Absolutely not! What this book is, is a source of enlightenment tailored to the advancement of the physically incarcerated. It is a guiding light, showing people how to "Outwit the System" — a system that's designed to stagnate and limit their potential for growth. This book is also for the physically free, yet, mentally incarcerated individuals that outnumber the physically incarcerated by a land slide.

A little about me; I came up in the pre-internet era. The men that had the most influence on our psyche were athletes, kingpins and pimps. By age 22, I was sentenced to 20 years in prison after being found guilty in a jury trial. I know exactly what it feels like to be betrayed in the courtroom by my own brother; to be betrayed by the system by being over-sentenced after an unfair trial. I know what it's like to see my mama cry on the stand before being sent off to go to some of the roughest, hardest prisons in the state of Georgia. I know what it's like to do over a decade behind prison walls, with your friends and family dying, while some dude is out there, raising your child. I know what it's like to make parole, then get sent back to prison after 21 months of being a model parolee based on what an officer said somebody else said you did, with that somebody never verifying the alleged facts at any hearing. I know what it's like to assert your constitutional rights before the parole board and for them to acknowledge it, and then through their actions, tell you, "Fuck your rights." I've seen the subtle racism within the system. I've seen defense attorneys play both sides and do what attorneys do within the system — attorn.

By being out for 21 months, then coming back in, I was able to notice the state of the incarcerated and even clearly see the wasted potential, and most importantly, the wasted time. What I noticed from going out there, or being out and coming back is that the biggest gift that you have in incarceration is free time. If you got plans, and ideas, things to test and try out, and you got plenty of time, do it. You don't have the advantage of 24 hours of free time in the free world unless you're a bum on the street. And with the technology that is out now, you can make it happen, as long as you got an internet connection and a smart device, anywhere in the world. This line stuck out to me — "Don't serve time, let the time serve you." Why not use the time to get a proper understanding of self and the skills needed to build wealth?

After doing 11 years, getting out of prison and seeing people doing worse than they were before I went into prison, I realized that I came out of prison in a better position — both appearance-wise and financially. It just says a lot about time and how you spend your time. If you don't have proper understanding of self and the proper knowledge of things that you can do to produce wealth, then it's as if you are locked up. Even if you're not physically locked, your mind is locked up and conditioned to something low, thus keeping you from reaching your full potential. When I first started my bid, after nine months in the county jail, I got shipped off to prison or Diagnostics, where you know everyone goes to get initiated into the prison system. They cut all your hair, make you strip down butt naked, and all the bullshit. It was an older prisoner that asked me how much time I had and basically gave me some insight into how to get through the time or make the time go by. He told me to just put in for a transfer every year. That way, I would be going to a different environment, and the time won't be so long, compared to how it would be if I had just stayed in the same spot until it was time to get out. The first advice I got involved mindset and how changing your environment can affect your time. That doesn't just apply to prison, but also applies to life in general. When a thing gets old, it becomes a drag; we don't want to have old bad habits or drag ourselves behind because of a lack of knowledge, causing us to be unproductive.

Later on in my bid, I got introduced to contraband behind the wall — cellphones, cigarettes and things of that nature. Once cigarettes were taken out of the system, this was my first chance of getting some money on the prison black market. Back then, we were using green dot to transfer the funds to prepaid Rush Cards. I was selling medicine cups of Bugler tobacco for $25, with 5 of those in a $4 pack; it was good profit. So, you could build your accounts off Bugler money. But it was the first thing. The contrabands can go from phones to tobacco, to the same drugs being distributed on streets. But now, with technology, you can be doing legal things inside; it doesn't have to be contraband. This reminds me of the words of a kingpin's father. He said, "My son could have been anything he wanted to be in life as smart and athletic he is, but he chose this." The message was that his millionaire son had the potential to be just as great as he was in the streets, if not better than what he was, but he chose the streets. So, we have to start choosing to do things that are going to make our parents proud and keep us from self-destruction. The system is not designed for you to be self-sufficient; the system wants you to have to rely on it, whether through you're coming back and forth to jail, or through the medical system. The system is in place to monetize off you. They have things like 60Days In and Lock Up, where these people make money off of you or someone else being in jail or prison. How can you spend all this time in a place where other people who haven't even spent one day there are making money off your time while you aren't?

Now, we gotta start monetizing our time. Regardless of whatever we spend time on, we should be able to pull the money out. When you go to jail or prison, you're spending a whole lot of time within the system, which in essence is a business. The whole Crime and Punishment thing has an underlying reason which is to profit. Your people have to get on a road and drive for hours, just to get to see you for a few hours. They had to get searched, and there's all that time away from your children. For you and your people to go through all that, you got to be able to get something out of it or find a way to get something out of it. You just can't be losing and not get something out of it.

I was doing fairly well before I had to come back on a parole violation, but I've come to accept that everything happens for a reason. If it wasn't for me coming back to prison on a parole violation, I wouldn't have ever written this book. I would never have been able to share any insight. Time is of the essence. I created the online fitness business, which I had already started before I came in, but the website, drop shipping, the branding — all of this stuff, I did in prison. I also learned about the stock market, forex and crypto. I learned how to trade in prison. I actually did these things in prison. If you learn these high-value skills and all these things behind the wall, you'll be able to create or start your online store. If you don't want to start an online store, you can learn how to trade and understand the stock market; you can get money anywhere in the world, and you will never have to worry about you being a convicted felon. You don't have to sign nobody's application because you're self-made from behind the wall.

Honestly, there are some six-figure prisoners doing it on contraband, but I'm not talking about doing that, because the thing about doing it on contraband is, the contraband is a stepping stone; you're not going to follow that path when you get out of jail. If you set the habit of always having to break a rule to get your money, nine times out of ten, if you don't have nothing in place to do the right thing, when you get out, you're most likely to break some more rules to keep making money when you get out. And that's going to lead you to come back.

The best thing we can do now, being behind the wall is to use whatever we can as a stepping stone that will benefit us in the future. We never have to come back again. We'll have the skills to build our family and skills to pass on to our loved ones. We can start building generational wealth from prison. The interesting thing is, the things I speak on are universal; anybody can apply these principles. But I'm focused on the people who come from where I'm from, or rather, the people who have the best opportunity and the most advantage when it comes to time. When you're in prison, you have the biggest advantage when it comes to time;

you have the biggest advantage when it comes to responsibility because when you're free, you have bills and all kinds of responsibilities that require your time, and clearly, you don't have those responsibilities in prison. So, if you are able to accumulate any type of money and you're able to put that towards something that can have you ahead of the curve when you get out, then guess what? You turned a bad situation into a marvelous situation. You found the seed of equivalent benefit as Napoleon Hill would say in his book, "Outwitting the Devil." Actually, that's what this book is about — outwitting the system that was designed to break you by using the time the system gave you to build you, to build your family, and to build your community.

This is how we're doing it. This book lays the foundation that you need to be self-sufficient, no matter where you are in life. As long as you have the will, the way will be made for you to make something happen. Regardless of your situation, you can get rich.

FIRST QUARTER

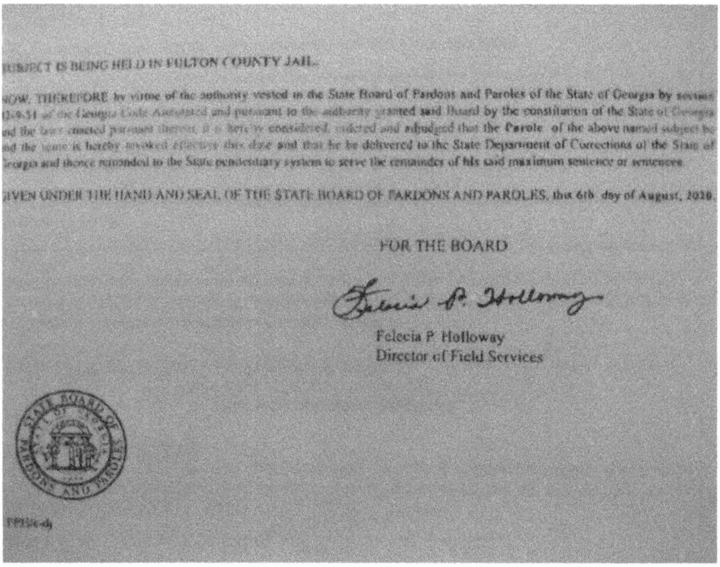

SUBJECT IS BEING HELD IN FULTON COUNTY JAIL.

NOW, THEREFORE by virtue of the authority vested in the State Board of Pardons and Paroles of the State of Georgia by section 42-9-51 of the Georgia Code Annotated and pursuant to the authority granted said Board by the constitution of the State of Georgia and the laws enacted pursuant thereto, it is hereby considered, ordered and adjudged that the **Parole** of the above named subject be and the same is hereby revoked effective this date and that he be delivered to the State Department of Corrections of the State of Georgia and thence remanded to the State penitentiary system to serve the remainder of his said maximum sentence or sentences.

GIVEN UNDER THE HAND AND SEAL OF THE STATE BOARD OF PARDONS AND PAROLES, this 6th day of August, 2020.

FOR THE BOARD

Felecia P. Holloway
Director of Field Services

STATE BOARD OF PARDONS AND PAROLES

FREE GAME

TOUGH TIMES DON'T LAST TOUGH PEOPLE DO

THE PRINCE OF DARKNESS

A lot of us don't know about the history of our race of people when it comes to success and creating and sustaining wealth. Before the 20th century, we were the most resilient race of people known to mankind. Very few of us know about Jeremiah Hamilton and how he was the first black millionaire on Wall Street during slavery. I'll give a brief history. This is not a history book, but I want to shed light on a few points and a few of our pioneers when it comes to financial success and in doing what you have to do in whatever situation to make it work for you and come out on top. We'll go back to the 1800s, where a man, Jeremiah Hamilton, made the most of his opportunities to accumulate wealth and ended up as Wall Street's first black millionaire. This man started as a "criminal." At the time, we had people of our race basically hustling, scamming and doing what they had to do to get to where they were trying to go, and turn negatives into positives. From where Hamilton started out, he became the first black millionaire on Wall Street, in the 1800s — not 1900s, not 2000s, but in the 1800s. Now, ponder on that.

Black millionaire, Jeremiah Hamilton, was a real estate investor with an estimated net worth of 2 million dollars, which is equal to 250 million today. He operated in an era when Wall Street was all white, but they had no choice but to respect him. Even Cornelius Vanderbilt, who was one of the richest people of the 19th century and in American history respected him; it's major that he was respected by this man in the 1800s. He got most of his money from white businesses in an era of not only Jim Crow, but also with full blown racism - slavery times - and that's what makes Hamilton such a historic figure; the fact that he was able to amass his wealth from predominantly white businesses during a racially charged period in America. Hamilton was called derogatory names, such as Nigger Hamilton and the Prince of Darkness.

In spite of the negative monikers, brokers and merchants rushed to do business with him. When he was 21 years old, he had a counterfeit coin operation coming from Haiti to New York City, and as soon as he was busted by the Haitian authorities, Hamilton went into hiding. White publications and black publications, cursed him for undermining the currency of the world's first entirely black republic. Despite that there were white merchants behind his operation, Hamilton never snitched or gave up his co-conspirators. Regardless of the situation, he had a plan or strategy to make money.

In the late 1830s, Hamilton bought insurance policies on ships that he purposely destroyed, and then used that money to purchase 47 plots of land in New York. He put more than $10 million in today's money in real estate, but amidst the panic of 1837, he got into serious financial trouble. Luckily for him, there was new financial legislation in the bankruptcy laws that allowed him to escape his creditors and come out ahead. By 1860, Hamilton was pulling funds, which in modern day terms, would be considered a hedge fund, where investors deposited money to invest on their behalf. The pool of money would allow Hamilton to borrow more money so that he would be able to invest a larger sum in the stock market. Hamilton made the decision on what stocks to buy and what stocks to sell. He was risking other people's savings to speculate pretty much on everything, and that's exactly what hedge funds do today. Hamilton was so successful, he amassed a gigantic fortune. He owned a massive portfolio of stocks, real estate, and eventually, he became Wall Street's first black millionaire with a house sitting on 276 acres of land in the 1800s.

Jeremiah Hamilton lived by the principle of OPM way before the acronym was widespread in the financial world. He passed away in May of 1875. Not really sure of his exact birthdate, but he passed in 1875, decades before the Negro or Black Wall Street existed. At the time of his death in 1875, Hamilton was the richest non-white man in America. If he did it then, indeed, you can do it now.

NEGRO WALLSTREET

Ottawa Gurley, aka, O.W., was a 20th century black educator, entrepreneur and land owner who was born to enslaved Africans. In 1889, after deciding to leave a position held with the Grover Cleveland presidential administration, O.W. moved from his home state of Arkansas, to Perry, Oklahoma, in order to participate in the Oklahoma Land Grab of 1889. Mr. Gurley, together with his wife, Emma, relocated to Tulsa to seize economic opportunities resulting from the city's multiracial population boom. Once there, he purchased a 40-acre tract of undeveloped land where he put a grocery store on a dirt road that ran just north of the train tracks. The 40 acres that Black Wall Street established was purchased by this great entrepreneur, Mr. O.W. Gurley, who later forged a partnership with fellow Black businessman, John the Baptist Stradford, also known as JB, who shared a general distrust of whites and chose to go by their initials instead of their first names. This action was a form of silent protest, because men in the south were customarily addressed by their surnames, while boys, by their first names. Sadly, adults were often addressed by their first names by white men as a form of emasculation. By using their initials, JB and OW circumvented this practice.

OW and JB occasionally shared different opinions. For example, while OW subscribed to the philosophies of African American educator Booker T. Washington, JB was more into the radical views of Civil Rights Activist W.E.B Dubois. Despite the differences, the two men worked together to develop an all-black district in Tulsa, Oklahoma, which developed into Black Wall Street. These two great entrepreneurs sub-divided this land into housing zones, retail lots, alleys and streets, all of which are exclusively available to other African Americans who would fear lynching and other racial harms. We cannot emphasize enough the fact that these two gentlemen established a booming and thriving economy just a few short years after slavery. After slavery, many black people had absolutely nowhere to go, and it was as if they almost created something out of nothing. After OW built several squares, he did two-story brick boarding houses, near his grocery stores. He called the street on which he set the structures Greenwood Avenue, after the Mississippi town from where many of his early residents came from.

Before long, the entire area became known as Greenwood; it soon became the site for a school, as well as an African Methodist Episcopal Church. But OW's greatest project was the Gurley hotel, whose high quality rivaled that of the finest white hotels in the state. As hundreds of African Americans migrated to Greenwood for the oil boom, OW and JB became increasingly wealthy, with OW having a net worth of $150,000 which is $3.6 million adjusted for inflation today. This great pioneer and entrepreneur leveraged his fortune to open a black masonic lodge and employment agency, while bankrolling efforts to resist black voter suppression in the state. This man was certainly a visionary.

OW Gurly was appointed as Sheriff deputy by the city of Tulsa, Oklahoma. Taking note of his success, white developers began to emulate OW and JB and began to purchase plots of land located north of the railroad tracks; they would then sell the plots back to members of the black community. By 1905, a black doctor and a black dentist had launched practices there. The creation of more schools, several hardware stores and Baptist Church soon followed. As segregation grew stronger, Greenwood's Black Business District thrived mainly because residents put their purchasing dollars back into the local economy. The dollar circulated amongst Black Wall Street's Greenwood District anywhere from 36 to 100 times before leaving the community, making them among the most powerful ever to exist. This determined entrepreneur has set the groundwork for us to follow. Black Wall Street was the most respected and highly-favored land for blacks in America. If they did it, then we can do it now.

RICHEST MAN EVER

Today's biggest fortunes barely register when compared to the richest people in history for millennia. These titles belong to royalty because they were not burdened by taxation and bureaucracy. These monarchs could accrue wealth unhindered. Among them are Augustus Caesar and Cleopatra, but there was one individual whose wealth topped all the rest. Mansa Musa Mansa Musa, whose name translates to Musa the Sultan was not only the richest man in Mali, he was the richest person in human history.

Details of Musa are somewhat scarce because he lived during the 14th century, but a few facts are certain. First of all, he wasn't born royalty. He was appointed deputy when Malian King Abu Bakar II left for a religious pilgrimage along the Atlantic Ocean and never returned. According to the laws of their kingdom, this made Musa their de facto king. Musa's ascension to the throne in 1312 came at a very important time in history. The Late Middle Ages were marked by population decline and unrest in Europe; the entire continent was suffering from famine, the Black Plague and political revolution. At the same time, North Africa was becoming a hub for commerce and industry. At this time, Musa came to power and took advantage of the economic stability in his region, but wasn't merely opportunistic. He inherited a country that was rich in natural reserves. Salt and gold were in abundance in Mali, and he soon became a successful merchant. In addition to his magisterial duties, he traded his gold all across Africa and Asia, establishing Timbuktu as the epicenter for commerce in the region.

Before his involvement, Timbuktu was barely established as a permanent settlement, but after renovation, the city had a constant stream of camels passing through each laden with more than 200 pounds of either salt or gold. To this day, the salt trade is robust in Timbuktu and still serves as a commercial hub more than 700 years later.

In addition to the economic gains, Musa oversaw the construction of Timbuktu's most iconic landmark — the Great Mosque of D'Jenne. As a devout Muslim, it was important to us that he paid tribute to his faith with his newfound power. D'Jenne mosque is made entirely from Adobe, and is considered by many architects to be one of the greatest achievements of the Sudano Sahelian. For the architectural style, Musa brought in architects from Southern Spain and across the Muslim nations to complete the project. The massive religious complex is the cultural center of Timbuktu, and was recently recognized as a UNESCO World Heritage site.

But beyond architectural achievements, Musa's rule saw huge diplomatic gains, using minimal force. He expanded the Malian Empire to include modern day Senegal, Gambia, Guinea, Burkina Faso, Mali, Niger, Nigeria and Chad. This is a particularly epic feat given that Musa only ruled for 25 years. In that time, his empire more than tripled. Many of the territories joined Mali willingly because of the relatively high quality of life afforded to its citizens. The wealth of his empire had a positive effect on the economic standing of his subjects. But when push came to shove, Musa was not afraid to use force. His fortune afforded him a massive and well-equipped military, which he used on numerous occasions, ultimately conquering 24 major cities in his lifetime. Musa never lost the battle in his life, which caused both Mali and his fortune to multiply fairly. Mansa Musa had an incredible fortune, but it wasn't until 1324 that the world learned exactly how obvious it was.

As a Muslim, he was obligated to go to Hajj or pilgrimage to Mecca in present day Saudi Arabia. The Quran states that all able-bodied practitioners of Islam should visit the holy site at least once in their lifetime. Though it was treacherous to travel such a long journey in the 1300s, Musa was determined to make the 4000-mile journey. As you can imagine, Musa didn't travel alone; he arranged for the most impressive caravan in human history to accompany him on his journey. Musa made his pilgrimage between 1324 and 1325. His procession reportedly included 60,000 men all wearing brocaded Persian silk, including 12,000 slaves who each carried four pounds of gold bars, and Harold's dressed in silks, who bought gold stamps organized horses and handle bags. Musa provided all necessities for the procession, feeding the entire company of men and animals. Those animals included 80 cannibals, which carried 50 to 300 pounds of gold dust. He also gave the goat to the poor he met along his route. Musa not only gave to the cities he passed on the way to Mecca, including Cairo and Medina, but also traded Grove for souvenirs. It was reported that he built a mosque every Friday. These numbers have been corroborated by eyewitnesses who were in awe of his wealth and generosity. For Musa, this was the trip of a lifetime, and he spared no expense. He was later interviewed by a Malian historian. His equipment and furnishings were carried by 12,000 private slave women wearing gowns of brocade and Yemeni silk. It is known that Musa visited with heads of state on his journey, but most famously, he met with Al Malik Al Nasir, the ruler of Egypt. The two kings commiserated on the challenges of royal life and traded business secrets. Their revelry went on for hours, and in the end, Musa made a powerful ally and trade partner.

Musa spread gold throughout his journey as a gift to the poor and those who accommodated him, He also gave a high amount during his stay in Cairo. However, Musa's generous actions inadvertently disrupted the economies of the region through which he passed in the cities of Cairo, Medina and Mecca. The sudden influx of gold devalued it for the next decade. Prices of goods and wares greatly inflated to rectify the gold market. On his way back from Mecca, Musa borrowed all the gold he could carry from moneylenders in Cairo at high interest. This is the only time recorded in history that one man directly controlled the price of gold in the Mediterranean. Upon reaching Mecca, Musa was focused on his religious faith, while his attendants and slaves continued to distribute his wealth. He spent weeks in prayer and formal ceremonies across the city. This part of his life was marked by discipline rather than excess during his long return journey from Mecca in 1325. Musa heard news that his army had recaptured the strategically important city of Gao.

When Mansa Musa returned, he brought back many Arabian scholars and architects. The conquering of Gao was seemingly effortless for Musa but it helped cement his reputation as a fearless and invincible leader. Musa's legacy continued as he began to focus on education. Upon his return, the University of South Korean Timbuktu was re-staffed with jurists, astronomers and mathematicians. The university became a center of learning and culture, drawing Muslim scholars from around Africa and the Middle East to Timbuktu. By the end of Mansa Musa's reign, the Suncor University had been converted into a fully-staffed university with the largest collection of books in Africa. Although it is difficult to adjust wealth to match modern day billionaires, economists had estimated his net worth at an unbelievable $400 billion. To put that in perspective, the richest person in the world is Jeff Bezos, who has amassed a fortune of $109 billion through the success of amazon.com. He's closely followed by Bill Gates and Warren Buffett, who each have about $90 billion. They made their fortunes in technology in the stock market, respectively. This means that no one in the world has even a quarter of Musa's massive fortune. The closest historical equivalent is John Rockefeller, whose adjusted fortune is about $340 billion. He amassed his fortune through the US oil company and various other industrial ventures. But even then, Rockefeller's net worth is a full $60 billion short of Mansa Musa's. Musa was one of the most influential and powerful people in human history. In all seven continents, since his death, no one has even come close to breaking his record. He still stands as the wealthiest person in human history.

Under Mansa Musa, it could be said that the Mali Empire consolidated its glory and power, and reached its end. It was through him that faith in one God took precedence, and Islam became the religion of state across the whole land. Even though it was confined to the elite and not practiced by the masses, it is an account. The structure of the Empire nevertheless took shape, laying the foundation for the others who were to follow. We can't talk about trading and wealth without mentioning Mansa Musa. Our community is way behind the example set by this great king. It's time for us to catch up.

Under Mansa Musa, Mali became one of the major centers of Islamic scholarship under a group of people who for centuries had been persecuted for their pursuit of knowledge.

HISTORY OF FOREX

So, where did it begin? Well, in the beginning, we had a bartering system where people would exchange goods and services with each other, depending on the value that they put on them. Then we exchanged commodities as a measure of value, and then that became done into coins or coins that were made of gold, silver and other materials. Eventually, that turned into a standard system for buying and selling goods and services.

After that, what we had was a currency. So, out of the Golden silver coins that were deposited in banks, these banks issued promissory notes, which were termed as a currency for the gold that were held, so they gave out notes as a promise to pay, based on the gold that was coins and the silver that was stored in the bank, and that created a gold standard for the currency backed by the bank that held gold. You'd have the notes, and your notes would be exchanged for gold and silver in the bank.

After World War II, we had an organization called IMF; it created a monetary policy, and all the currencies around the world were pegged to the dollar. The dollar was also pegged to gold at $35 an ounce on the weight of the gold. We had this standard for a while, then we moved on from there, and in 1970s, Richard Nixon, the president of the USA took the dollar off the gold standard. So, the link between the two was now canceled. The currency was now to be printed in large quantities, leading to a lot more currency than there was gold. A lot of many notes were printed. But we moved on from there in the modern system, after 1973, IMF created a system of international currency exchange, but that exchange was only available between the banks. Therefore, only very large amounts of currency were being exchanged.

In the 90s, when technology came in, we had the internet and widespread use of computers. With that technology, we had advancements, and in 1994, the countries around the world floated their currencies on the market. As time went on, in 1998, a currency trading system was introduced in the USA. The market opened up for anyone to trade currencies at the spot market prices for those currencies, and as that became available, we had more adoption, as well as institutions and other smaller companies. As that adoption grew, the forex market grew into the biggest market in the world; it is now several trillion dollars a day in volume. Most of the trading going on through the technology, the mass adoption and those trading systems are all pretty much online. So that's where we are right now, and that's far from where we started. We started with basics of bartering commodities, and then coins turned into storage of gold, which were given out through notes, promises and IOUs. Then we had all the currencies linked to the dollar after the war, and then the dollar linked to gold. Afterwards, dollar was taken off the gold system, and then technology created a market that's almost the biggest in the world. There are massive opportunities for anyone to trade those currencies; opportunities that weren't available to the pimps or heroin and crack kingpins of the 70's, 80's and even 90's.

SECOND QUARTER

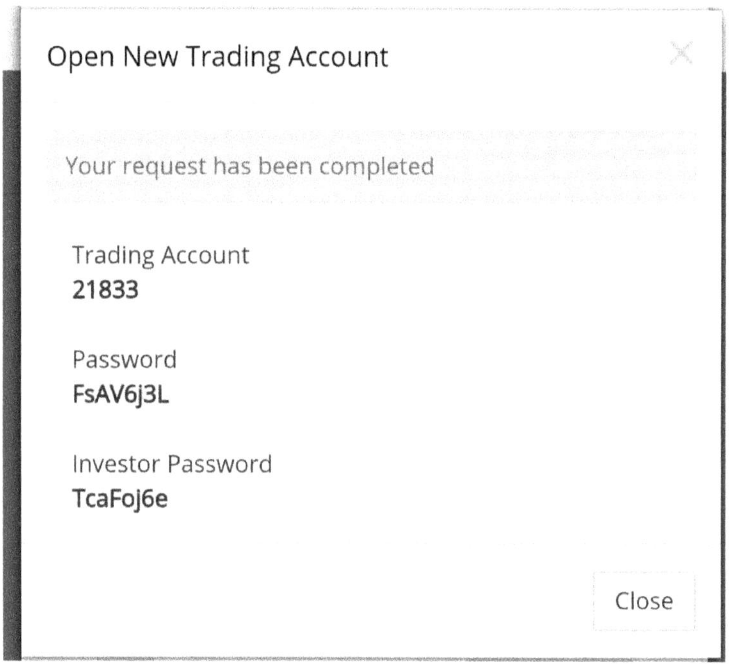
Open New Trading Account
Your request has been completed
Trading Account
21833
Password
FsAV6j3L
Investor Password
TcaFoj6e
Close

FREE GAME

EARN WHILE YOU LEARN YOUR LESSON

THE ECONOMICS OF FOREX

The foreign exchange market (forex) is one of the most influential markets in the world. New York Stock Exchange, the NASDAQ and the Tokyo Stock Exchange are three largest secure markets in the world. They have a combined daily trading volume of around $300 billion each day and the foreign exchange market has a daily trading volume of around $6.6 trillion a day according to the Bank for International Settlements, which is basically the central bank of central banks.

Why is forex market flooded with cash? Well, each country has a comparative advantage or are a bit more specialized in the goods and services they produce. Chinese iPhone manufacturers aren't interested in being paid Euros, and German car manufacturers aren't interested in the Chinese Yen, so, they trade currencies. This makes a secondary market because suddenly, you're not only exchanging cars and phones, but Euros and Yen as well.

The foreign exchange market has grown so large because global trade has grown to require it. Most people really don't have that much exposure to the foreign exchange market outside of trading currencies when they go on holidays or perhaps do some online shopping through a website that doesn't automatically convert to a local currency. All of those types of retail transactions make up a tiny percentage of the total foreign exchange market. The real players are companies, investment firms and governments, all of which play an equal influential role. Businesses are the easiest to understand. If they want to open up a new store in a new country, they are going to need to transfer money to that country and convert it to the local currency in order to buy cars or pay workers, for supplies, and expenses. This is all pretty straightforward and easy to understand. However, there is foreign exchange risk that can cause the company to lose money if the foreign dollar crumbles. So, they need a hero who is willing to take on the risk for them. This brings us to the investor. Investors love the foreign exchange market or forex market because of the potential for returns. It signifies that this was done through financial instruments called derivatives. And when you hear a word titled derivatives, just remember they are kind of just a made-up thing that has their value derived from some other asset. What investors do is basically make a bet with the company. If the value of the foreign currency goes up relative to the currency in your home market, pay me; if the foreign currency goes down, I pay. Just remember that speculative investors want to take on risk, for potential profits, and a normal international business wants to get rid of any foreign exchange risks, even if it means that it might otherwise miss out on some speculative profits. A risk in the market is nothing compared to the risks we've taken with our lives and freedom for peanuts. Once you learn this skillset, you've got it for life without having to risk being sentenced to life.

TRADERS AND BROKERS

We're going to get into the differences between retail traders and institutional traders. If you don't trade for institutions or aren't trading for a bank, then you're probably not managing a lot of capital or a lot of people's capital, so it means you're pretty much a retail trader. So, the retail trader is an individual investor who buys and sells securities on their own accounts. If you're trading for yourself on apps like Metatrader, WeBull, or Robinhood personally for you, that makes you a retail investor. An institutional trader is a trader who buys and sells securities for accounts that they manage; they do it for organizations like banks, insurance companies, or for retirement funds, or hedge funds. A retail trader usually gets their education by searching on the internet; they make money in their spare time, or they become full time traders and enjoy the flexibility. You can also learn how to do all sorts of things on YouTube. It's one of the world's biggest educational sources.

Moving to the institutional side, these traders will typically get an economics, math or finance degree from college before getting a job at a finance institution. They often start their careers as junior analysts, and then they work their ways to become fund managers or senior fund manager over the years. Retail traders focus on indicators, price patterns, and technical systems, or basically read and react to the market. Institutional traders focus more on fundamental systems, the news, trading psychology, and market sentiment or what kind of feel they have for the market. If you're not confident in what to do, it's going to be hard to do it; these institutional traders have got the psychology down big time. They've mastered their psychology, and that's how they're able to manage these accounts. What are these institutional funds? Retail traders buy and sell stocks — around like 100 shares. Institutional traders engage in block trades, which is an order to buy or sell 10,000 or more shares at a time.

Institutions are the largest force behind supply and demand in securities markets. They perform the majority of trades on major exchanges, and greatly influence the prices. Retail traders invest in stocks, bonds or futures. Institutional traders have the same thing, just that retail traders have minimal access to IPOs, while institutional traders have access to IPOs. When you trade for yourself, you'll see the fees, so you'll know. Institution traders don't pay fees to trade; they charge fees to trade. Institutional investors do not use their own money, but rather, invest other people's money on their behalf. On the other hand, retail investors invest for themselves, offering in a brokerage or retirement account. If you're not trading like institutions, they don't trade any differently; they just got more money.

Next, we're going to go over how retail traders fund their trading account. The way this is done is through a broker. The first thing that you should know about a broker is that they give you leverage. Basically, leverage is like a broker fronting you money. What you have to understand is that when you are trading the Forex market to actually place trades, know that you need thousands and thousands of dollars. The way that middle-class people are able to benefit from the foreign exchange market is by using something called leverage. Let's just say you had $1 and the broker gives you 1:50 leverage, that means you'll really be trading like you have $50 in your account, and that's like the simplest way I can explain. If your broker has a one to 500 leverage, if you have $1, you really can trade like you have $500 in your account. The more money you have, multiply it by whatever your leverage is. Depending on what that leverage is, you're able to trade as if you have more money in your account. And that's how middle-class people are able to make a lot of money inside of the foreign exchange market. If we didn't have leverage, and we only had $10 to put a trading account, that $10 probably would not even be able to make one trade off. If you are in the U.S., all US brokers have regulations to where you can't get more than 1:50 leverage. One to fifty is a very small leverage if you have a small amount to deposit, so it doesn't really allow you to make much money. Foreign brokers allow much more leverage than the U.S. In order to use a foreign broker, you need to be 18 years old, with some form of ID and also need to have a bill in your name. You basically sign up for a broker with a minimum of $10, and you can have a one to 500 leverage, which most brokers outside of the US do have; that's the maximum, and you will be able to trade as if you have $5000. Hugo's Way is the least restrictive broker to sign up with. Some foreign brokers offer up to one to one thousand leverage. Different brokers offer different options as to leverage and what you can trade, such as crypto, indices, exotics, futures, stocks and commodities. It's not only forex pairs.

STOCKS VS FOREX

An advantage of the stock market is that there's a lot of stocks, and thousands and thousands of stocks that you can look up on. There are certain fundamental investment opportunities here based on what those companies are doing. And that's very cool for people who are looking for a wide range of things to trade or get involved with, all with financial markets. Another is that there is a lot of long-term growth potentials in the company. According to long-term standards, if a company is actually making money, then theoretically, they should go up in value. For example, companies like Apple, Costco, and Coca Cola that make money, grow and add more profit to their balance sheet over the long term. So, that is a great long-term investor with stocks. Investing the Canadian or U.S. dollar isn't as interesting long-term.

This next point is that there's a lot of volatility for people interested in day trading. The stock market gets going at 9:30am EST in the U.S.; other countries have different times that's usually sometime in the morning as well. Starting Monday, at 9:30, the US market spikes like crazy as people enter and rush to buy or sell stock. So, that can be really good for those traders who want those high-paced big moves in the markets. Notice that there's a lot of opportunity for Swing

Trading. So, whatever you want to do in the stock market, there is diversity. Next up is, there is stock investment. A currency like the US dollar literally has millions of variables that make the price go up or down in value. Now, with stock, there's still a ton of variables, but there's potentially less to look at things like CEO, revenues, long-term performance of a company when it comes to pricing stock, but it's a lot less than the macro trends of the world economy that comes into play with the US dollar. Stocks trading also has zero commission models. The cons of the stock market are that stock can go to $0 if a company goes bankrupt, whereas, a currency can almost never go down to $0. Stock market trading doesn't provide much leverage, and has less trading hours, so if your schedule isn't in alignment with these set hours, you'll miss opportunities in the market, but forex on the other hand is a 24/7 market where you can find a market around the world that is open and volatile at times, and more in tune with your schedule.

In trading stocks and forex, it is important to note that the stock market is a centralized market, whereas, the forex market is a decentralized market. For this reason, one thing we have to take note of is that there is no perfect way to measure the amount of volume actually being traded in the forex market. Even though volume is available from most Forex brokers, it's derived from the filters on data stream. Those numbers don't represent the total worldwide market volume. They are only partially meaningful and helpful, as they represent a proportional measure of the total volume being traded worldwide.

Another noteworthy point is that there is no uptake rule in the forex market. What this means is that the exchange requires that every short sale transaction entered at a price that is higher than the price of the previous trade. That's why it's not convenient to short sell a security for retail traders, and most are not used to short selling but there is no such restriction in the forex market. So, forex traders can make profits easily, in both directions. If we think a currency will increase in value, we can buy it. If we think it will decrease, we can sell it. With a market this large, finding a buyer when we are selling, and a seller when we are buying is much easier than in other markets.

Theoretically, stock prices can go up indefinitely, as long as the earnings keep growing. Likewise, when a company has financial problems, or if it's close to bankruptcy, the price can be close to zero. But in the forex market, this concept is different because when we are buying a currency, we are simply buying its strength in relation to another currency. The chart that we see on a stock chart is its price, but on the Forex chart, it's an exchange rate. Obviously, it makes no sense if we spend US dollar to buy the US dollar, so in order to buy the US dollar, we must be selling some other currencies in exchange for it. For this reason, the forex market is volatile in the short term, because every currency is constantly being compared with other currencies.

Lastly, is the number of trading alternatives available. The Forex market has very few compared to the thousands found in the stock market. This concentration on a few currency pairs gives us the advantage of being able to specialize and follow because rather than having to pick between a thousand stocks to find the best value, the only thing forex traders need to do was keep up with the political and economic news. For instance, most scalpers will only trade their own because of its high liquidity and become very expert on just one pair. Stock traders can decide to specialize just in a few very liquid stocks such as Bank of America or Bank of China. However, those strategies typically involve having to monitor the major equity index, such as the S&P 500 and the US, or the Hang Seng Index in Hong Kong, which makes the setup more complicated.

So, which is better? Stocks or Forex? It would be unfair to make an absolute judgment in favor of either one. It really depends on our character and preferences. Some traders naturally feel more comfortable with stocks, while others, with Forex. For the long-term investors, stocks may be a better choice because they can make spectacular price moves, and entries don't need to be so precise. There's more forgiveness in getting in a bit too early or too late for example, but for traders looking to do short-term or medium-term trading, forex with higher levels of leverage and liquidity available should be a serious consideration. Moreover, it also requires less capital, and the scanning and filtering process is simpler.

CRYPTO

Cryptocurrency like Bitcoin, Ethereum, Ripple, LiteCoin, and Solana are traded and invested in on the market. But a lot of people are now publicly very transfixed on Bitcoin, because that's the big one. Bitcoin has been in our system for over 10 years. Loads of things have happened, and there's so many misconceptions about it. So, let's go back to where it all started — around 2008, which was the big financial crash. Back then, the basic premise was that the bank had cocked up. At the time, we had a big recession. So, how did Bitcoin come to be? A group of people - a group of programmers - got together under the pseudonym of Satoshi Nakamoto, and they basically came up with this concept — some may disagree. The problem was, why do we need a bank or third parties for in order for two different people to pay each other? So, if I were to buy something from you, or as you bought your equipment off me, why do we need to trust Santander or NatWest to swap that money between our clients when we can just do that ourselves? So that was kind of where it all came around. Bitcoin was designed to create a mechanism where I can pay you directly. It's a direct thing, and that's the whole premise of what the technology advocates; it's basically cash, but a digital version. It was exactly that a digital cash. The same way I could give you cash now and no one else needs to get involved. they created an online version of that same process. Up until then, and even now, the majority requires a bank of government investment to do that transaction. This is where blockchain technology was then created — the cool underlying technology behind all this. I'll explain what this is in a later chapter but blockchain technology really, is much more simple than people want to care for. It's simply just blocks of information, critical information and not money. So, the way the blockchain works with Bitcoin is, instead of being a bank, it swaps the money between us — the blockchain. It kind of operates a little bit like a big Excel sheet or a big spreadsheet that everyone can see. But once a record has been put on them, it can never change, so you can never say that the money didn't go. If I sent you one Bitcoin, the whole Bitcoin blockchain would publicly declare that this address, sent this coin to that address, and it's stamped forever. So, one of the misconceptions of Bitcoin is that it's this anonymous, crazy currency that can just make money disappear. The reality of it is, it's one of the most traceable data records, and there is a transparent information stamp. Yeah, the best way to kind of think about it is a little bit like the internet; but then, if you mention the internet as the cool underlying technology upon which eBay, Amazon, Microsoft and Facebook work, some wouldn't say that Facebook is the internet. I mean, it might be for a lot of people, but well, I'm just using that analogy, explaining that it's the same for the blockchain. The internet is the underlying technology that Amazon, Microsoft, and Facebook operate on, and it's the same with Blockchain/crypto/Bitcoin.

An alt coin is an alternative coin; so, technically speaking, an alt coin is any coin that is not Bitcoin. Bitcoin was the first cryptocurrency, and all the rest of them have inherited the name, cryptocurrencies. There are a lot of coins out there, so this kind of comes around again from this kind of big run in 2017, where there was a big craze over the ICO; there's something called an ICO (initial coin offering). So, when a company launches on the stock market, it has an IPO - an initial public offering - where people can buy the shares in theory a little bit cheaper than where they think the business is going to go. So, in the crypto world, because the technology advanced before regulation, all the guys in the crypto world came up with this cool new thing called ICO, an initial coin offering, where they basically promise all of this, and you buy our coins at a certain price. So, if you kind of apply the same logic to the cryptos that you're investing in, what's the product? What does it do? Why is it a business problem? What does it fix? Is the technology good? Does it look like they've got a good marketing team and a good staff team? Is their location visible, and are they verifiable? So, as an investor, really think about cryptocurrencies and alt coins as you would any other investments.

Why would I choose Bitcoin over normal money? What you have to remember is, Bitcoin has been around 10 years now. There are a lot of people that have 10 grand in cash today. So, there's a lot of Bitcoin millionaires out there that put in a couple of hundred or thousand dollars that are now buying new cars, buying houses and buying equipment because they invested what to them was a very small amount of money.

But the beauty of it is, if you believe in this fundamental blockchain technology, Bitcoin is simply just an example. So effectively, what Bitcoin demonstrated was this kind of "screw-the-banks" system, "we will do it ourselves." That was the kind of ethos but ironically, with that technology that was created, there's just so many inherent advantages that it's been adopted commercially for more mainstream things. JPMorgan coin, for example, you can't buy it, and you can't get some of it. It's designed to settle international funds for various JPMorgan accounts. So, it's an internal thing for them, but it fundamentally runs on a similar baseline technology. Everything in the crypto market is traded in Bitcoin. These days, if bitcoin moves a lot, it goes up 10%. Typically, the smaller coins will move up by a larger percentage, because there's less money, but they generally follow each other. I noticed a link with when it was ether, and how the bitcoin price went up. The price went up; it was almost like they were joined. Bitcoin is so everything in the crypto world. These crypto tokens - these 2000 Crypto tokens - are all interchangeable. They're all interchangeable with Bitcoin; you can take 100 Raven coin and turn it into this much Bitcoin or vice versa with any of these coins. Bitcoin is the lead in all of that.

THIRD QUARTER

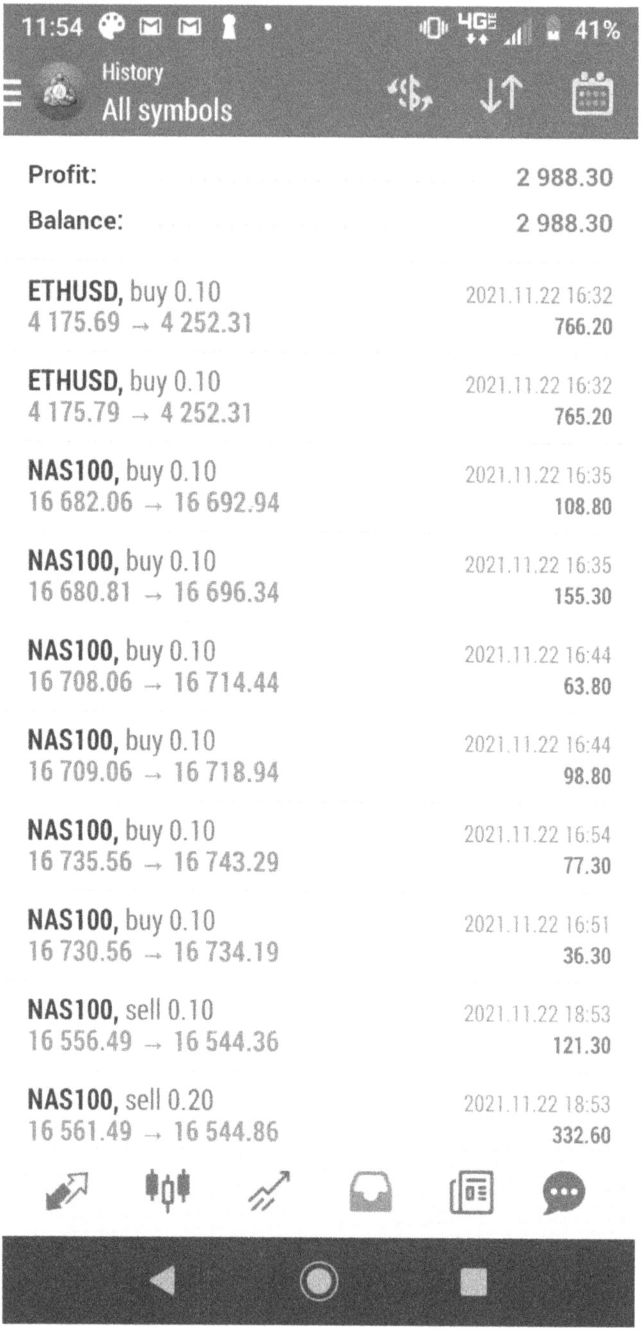

11:54 41%

History
All symbols

Profit: 2 988.30
Balance: 2 988.30

ETHUSD, buy 0.10 — 2021.11.22 16:32
4 175.69 → 4 252.31 — 766.20

ETHUSD, buy 0.10 — 2021.11.22 16:32
4 175.79 → 4 252.31 — 765.20

NAS100, buy 0.10 — 2021.11.22 16:35
16 682.06 → 16 692.94 — 108.80

NAS100, buy 0.10 — 2021.11.22 16:35
16 680.81 → 16 696.34 — 155.30

NAS100, buy 0.10 — 2021.11.22 16:44
16 708.06 → 16 714.44 — 63.80

NAS100, buy 0.10 — 2021.11.22 16:44
16 709.06 → 16 718.94 — 98.80

NAS100, buy 0.10 — 2021.11.22 16:54
16 735.56 → 16 743.29 — 77.30

NAS100, buy 0.10 — 2021.11.22 16:51
16 730.56 → 16 734.19 — 36.30

NAS100, sell 0.10 — 2021.11.22 18:53
16 556.49 → 16 544.36 — 121.30

NAS100, sell 0.20 — 2021.11.22 18:53
16 561.49 → 16 544.86 — 332.60

FREE GAME

LIFE DOESN'T HAVE TO BE FAIR IN ORDER FOR YOU TO SUCCEED

METAVERSE

So, in the simplest term, the metaverse is a virtual reality world. This is all on a computer basically, and it's all virtual in the metaverse. You could do tons of different things. You could interact with people, objects or buildings. Again, it's like a virtual game, but in this case, it's almost like playing a game of life inside of the computer. You could also own things inside of the metaverse. So, for example, you could own a plot of land and build a virtual building on that land. You could also own digital assets in that world as well. Those are called NFTs (non-fungible tokens). But just to simplify, you could own properties and digital assets in the Metaverse. I have to explain the concept of Metaverse because it's just not one place; there is not just one Metaverse, so if you think of our physical world, right, there's one planet all of us live in this planet. Well, the metaverse is not quite like that, because there's a bunch of different meta verses. I kind of think of it as multiple planets, and you get to choose which one you want to interact in.

There's a couple of ways to actually go inside of a metaverse. You could actually go to a website that takes you into one metaverse. You could also jump into a Metaverse using a virtual reality headset. Some are going to be eventually owned by big corporations like the one Facebook has, and the one Microsoft is putting together as well, and then there are going to be decentralized meta verses. Those are meta verses that are on the blockchain that no single company owns. Metaverse world kind of got a life from that experience we had in 2020 and beyond, where we just couldn't be physically at different locations and didn't want to travel at all. So, this is going to be the next level to that I think is going to be the norm. I think we're going to spend the majority of our days in the metaverse and less time in the real world. There's this website which is a marketplace for NFTs and virtual lands. There are also platforms like OpenSea. If you go to open c.io, you could press explore and see all kinds of different things.

So, virtual worlds are basically the different meta verses. And these are all the ones that are going to be decentralized. The most popular Metaverse is called Decentraland. The second one is called Sandbox. Decentraland and decentraland.org is the website for that. This is an entire virtual world where you could do all kinds of different things. With Decentraland, you could build your own avatar or your virtual character. You could jump into the game and start exploring. You could chat or even use your microphone to interact with other people. You could also use the map to see all kinds of different things with an overview of what's around you, and you could just teleport to any one location or event in a second. You don't actually have to walk over to a place. A lot of times you can teleport to the next place you want to go to. Decentraland also has its own marketplace on their website where you could actually browse and look at different things like NFTs that you could own. You could show them off or wear them within the game. They also have land here that you could buy, so you could actually look at a big overview of the map and buy any little parcel of land here in Decentraland. OpenSea also has a Decentraland collection here, where this works more like an eBay platform where you have the minimum bid, and you could bid on land and then compete in an auction kind of format. Some have buyers as well, where you could go ahead and browse this platform for buying land there. There's going to be a whole bunch of virtual experiences that you could have without leaving your home. And I think once this headset and other headsets really take off. It's going to make this very immersive experience right now. You need that virtual reality experience when you enter a metaverse. It's really not going to look great or really feel that immersive when you look at it on the computer. Once you jump in, in a VR world - what it's really designed to be - you're really going to be blown away. The second biggest one of all time is called Sandbox. Now, the Sandbox actually has a lot of traction, and even has people like Snoop Dogg doing concerts in that virtual world.

But in the meantime, you could explore these things on the computer, if you don't have a headset at all. And I should also mention inside of each metaverses, they do have their own currency. In Decentraland, their currency is called mana. You could actually buy this coin in places where they sell virtual currency. The virtual currency of Decentraland can be used to buy all kinds of events, activities and plots of land, These Metaverses typically have their own kind of economies and currencies. The currencies depend on the Metaverse that's chosen. A lot of these currencies can also be bought with regular money; for instance, I can buy mana with US Dollars, and then use mana to actually do things in the metaverse. This means that within Decentraland, I could actually buy things, events or land with Mana.

NFT

NFT stands for non-fungible token. Non-fungible means that something cannot be exchanged for another item because it is unique. For instance, one piece of art is not equal to another, as both have unique properties. Fungible items on the other hand can be exchanged for one another. For instance, $1 or bitcoin is always equal to another. NFTs are tokens that live on a blockchain and represent ownership of unique items. Why is that helpful? Well, tracking who owns a digital file is tricky, because it can be copied and distributed effortlessly. So how can you prove who was the original owner when everyone has an identical copy of the file and solve this problem? Imagine that you made a piece of digital art, essentially a JPEG on a computer, you can create or mint NFT out of this. The NFT that represents your art contains a bit of information about it, such as a unique fingerprint of the file, a token name or symbol. This token is then stored onto a blockchain, and you - the artist - become the owner. Now, you can sell the token by creating a transaction on the blockchain. The blockchain makes sure that this information can never be tampered with. It also allows you to track the current owner of a token for how much it has been sold in the past. It's important to note that the artwork itself is not stored within the NFT or the blockchain. Its attributes, such as the fingerprint or hash of the file, a token name, symbol or optionally, a link to a file would be posted on IPFS. Now, here's where NFTs become weird. When you buy an NFT that represents artwork, you don't get a physical copy of it most of the time. Everyone can download a copy for free. The NFT only represents ownership, and that is recorded in a blockchain, so nobody can tamper with it. Some NFTs just give you digital bragging rights, and to make it even weirder, while the token owner owns the original artwork, the creator of the NFT retains the copyright and the reproduction rates, so the artist can sell his original artwork as an NFT but he can still sell prints. Now aside from digital art, NFTs can also be used to sell concert tickets, domain names, rare in-game items, real estate, and basically anything that is unique and needs proof of ownership. For example, the founder of Twitter's first tweet was sold. Anyone can see that tweet on his profile, but now, only one person can own it, and that person paid over $2.9 million for it. Now, why are some NFTs worth millions? Well, their worth is determined by what people are willing to pay. If I'm willing to pay $100 for a particular NFT, then it's worth $100. Prices are driven by demand, so be careful. An expensive NFT becomes worthless if nobody wants to buy it. One more thing regarding how NFT'S work technically is, NFTs are essentially smart contracts that live on a blockchain. In this case, the contract stores the unique properties of the item and keeps track of current and previous owners. NFT can be programmed to get royalties to the creator every time it exchanges hands.

NFTs are a huge win for contemporary artists with the galleries and auction houses attached to NFT platforms. It is a form of social currency and digital form of expression.

Contemporary artists should take advantage of this technology. Artists and replication providers, should also tap in, as there is no excuse for them not to use the high market artwork infrastructure as an auction house. I'm looking at the home, wearing the clothes as a subconscious way to communicate to the world. Everything we do is communication. The homes we live in, clothes we wear, cars we drive are all a subconscious way we communicate to the world. Everything we do is communication.

BLOCKCHAIN

Nowadays, what is a blockchain? How do they work? What problems do they solve and how can they be used? Blockchain is a chain of blocks that contains information. It was originally described in 1981 by a group of researchers, and was originally intended to timestamp digital documents, so it's not possible to back-date or tamper with them; it's almost like a notary. However, it went by mostly unnoticed until it was adapted by Toshi Nakamoto in 2009. To create a digital cryptocurrency, Bitcoin or blockchain is a distributed ledger that is completely open to anyone. They have an interest interesting property. Once some data has been reported inside the blockchain, it becomes very difficult to change it. So how does that work? Well, let's take a closer look at a block. Each block contains some data, the hash of the block and the hash of the previous block. Things that are stored inside the block depend on the type of blockchain. The Bitcoin blockchain, for example, stores the details about a transaction, such as the sender, receiver, and the amount of coins. A block also has a hash which is like a fingerprint. It identifies a block and all of its contents, and it's almost as unique as a fingerprint. Once a block is created, its hash has been calculated as well. Changing something inside the block will cause the hash to change. So, in other words, hashes are very useful when you want to detect changes the blocks. If the fingerprint of a block changes, it is no longer the same block. The third element of each block is the hash of the previous block, and this effectively creates a chain of blocks. Now, let's say that you tamper with the second block, discuss the hash of the block to changes well. In turn, that will make block three and all falling blocks invalid because they no longer store a valid hash of the previous block. So, changing a single block, or following blocks using hashes is not enough to prevent tampering. Computers these days are very fast and can calculate hundreds of thousands of hashes per second. You can effectively tamper with a block and recalculate all the hashes of other blocks to make your blockchain valid again. To prevent this, blockchains have something that is called proof of work. It's a mechanism that slows down the creation of new blocks. In Bitcoin's case, it takes about 10 minutes to calculate the required proof of work and add a new block to the chain. This mechanism makes it very hard to tamper with the blocks because if you tamper with one block, you'll need to recalculate the proof of work for all the following blocks. So, the security of the blockchain comes from its creative use of hashing and the proof of work mechanism. But there is another way that blockchain secures themselves, and that is by being distributed instead of by using. A central entity Blockchain uses a peer-to-peer network and everyone is allowed to join. When someone joins these networks, it gets a full copy of the blockchain. The node can use this to verify that everything is still in order. When someone creates a new block, that block is sent to everyone on the network - each node - and verifies the block to make sure that it hasn't been tampered with. And if everything checks out, each node adds this book to the blockchain. All the nodes in this network create a consensus to agree on what blocks are valid and which aren't. Blocks that are tampered with will be rejected by other nodes in the network. So, to successfully tamper with a blockchain, you'd have to tamper with all the blocks on the chain, redo the proof of work for each block and take control of more than 50% of the p2p network. Only then will the tampered block become accepted by everyone else. This is almost impossible to do, as blockchains are also constantly evolving.

One of the most recent developments is the creation of smart contracts. These contracts are simple programs that are stored on the blockchain and can be used to automatically exchange coins based on certain conditions. More on smart contracts in a later chapter. The creation of blockchain technology piqued a lot of people's interest, and soon, others realized that this technology can be used for other things like storing medical records, digital notary, or even collecting taxes.

SMART CONTRACTS

Smart contracts are very popular nowadays. But what are they and what problems are they solve? Now, smart contracts are just like contracts in the real world. The only difference is that they are completely digital. In fact, a smart contract is actually stored inside of a blockchain. With smart contracts, we can build a system that doesn't require a third party. So, let's create a smart contract. We can program smart contracts to hold received funds until a certain goal is reached. The supporters of a project can now transfer their money to smart contract. If project gets fully funded, the contract automatically passes the funding to the creator of the project, and if the project fails to meet these goals, then the money automatically goes back to supporters. And because smart contracts are stored inside a blockchain, everything is completely distributed, and no one is in control of the money.

Why trust the smart contracts, you might ask? Well, because smart contracts are stored on a blockchain, and they possess some interesting properties — they are immutable and distributed. Being immutable means that once a smart contract is created, it can never be changed, so no one can go behind your back to tamper with the code of the contract. Being distributed means that the output of a contract is validated by everyone on the network. So, a single person cannot force the contract to release the funds because other people in the network will spot the attempt and mark them as invalid. Tampering with smart contracts becomes almost impossible. Smart contracts can be used for many different things outside of crowd-funding. Banks for example can use it to issue loans or to offer automatic payments, insurance companies could use it to process certain claims and postal companies can use it for payment on delivery. So, now, you might wonder where and how can I use smart contracts? For right now, there are a handful of blockchains who support smart contracts. The biggest one is Ethereum. This one was specifically created and designed to support smart contracts. Smart contracts can be programmed in a special programming language called solidity. This language was specifically created for Ethereum and uses a syntax that resembles JavaScript. It's also worth noting that Bitcoin also has support for smart contracts, although it's a lot more limited compared to Ethereum.

DEFI

The word Defi is short for decentralized finance.

What exactly is decentralized finance (Defi)?

Defi is a term for a variety of decentralized services that aim to replace our current centralized financial system. This decentralized service will enhance the opportunity to allow people who have been discriminated upon or people who live in the economy that does not facilitate the right kind of adoption that allow them to participate in the global economic movement right now.

Decentralized finance can solve so many issues with banking and non-banking, thus allowing people to come in and become their own bank. There are so many things right now that Defi brings to the table and my goal is to demystify a lot of this and make sure that you have a better understanding of what it is, how it works and how you can effectively utilize it.

Decentralized finance includes Bitcoin, as we have to talked about Bitcoin before in the chapter on crypto. Bitcoin is not controlled by any bank or any government, it is decentralized. It is one of the top decentralized projects in the market that can be sent to anyone at any time, it can be received by anybody who has a wallet for it to be sent into. Bitcoin is a decentralized asset but it has been coded in a way that it won't facilitate the right kind of adoption within Defi, so we need projects that can actually benefit us in the Defi space. The main network that the Defi is built on is Ethereum.

Defi is going to be huge, but we understand that bitcoins place right now isn't going to be in defi. Now before we go deeper into defi, I want to talk a little bit about centralized finance. Just like our traditional legacy system, all the services that we currently have right now rely on a centralized authority, like with banks, when we are talking about loans, and we are looking to get involved in real estate or things like that, everything we have now with our traditional legacy system is centralized. It has a central point of failure which makes them very vulnerable to different things like robberies, hacks, mismanagement, fraud, and corruption.

We have seen it happen so many times with big businesses where people just get to come in and embezzle things. While the people in accounting are not paying attention to this things or they are the ones involved, there is always these central points of failure within a company or within our traditional system that we have right now. That's the importance of having something like decentralized finance or the Defi system, because this system can absolutely bring an entire new wave of how money is moved, how money is managed, and also how systems are put in place to keep things honest and transparent.

When you think about the traditional system that we have right now, we have something like the Federal Reserve that is just printing a whole lot of money, and there's nothing we can do about it. It's just that they can print as much as they want and the government can ask for as much as they want. So knowing that we have a centralized entity like the Fed that can print as much money as they want at the push of a button, it is really important that we are very mindful of what we are dealing with right now, while we talk about these centralized entities, now the other thing about Defi is that we need to have the proper kind of components or define the word. Decentralized infrastructure needs to be laid out in front of you, so that you can have a better understanding of how this really works, what all this is and how we can actually utilize something like Etherium and V coin when it comes to defi.

Defi is very much a do it yourself platform with a decentralized program called dex or daps. Everybody calls it a different word but it is basically a smart contract which allows you to basically put code in place that removes all of the potential corruption in this so called management. This code, the smart contract will have certain protocols that have to be met and once they are put into play, there is no way to change or alter the system. It is immutable. So we trust that the code will continue to do what it's going to do without having any kind of weird mishap or any kind of corruption put into it.

We have to make sure that the code is being tested before it's been put into play. Etherium facilitates that with the smart contracts, blockchain and structure that it brings to the table so once we have a theory and a smart contract, we're good to go. Moving along into the other components of decentralized infrastructure we need decentralized money and this is where the stable coin starts to come into play because with Etherium, it's great, It's awesome, It's innovative, but it's volatile. Its price fluctuates up and down so that Ethereum can do a lot of things, but the volatility does bring a bit of an unstable aspect to the Defi system. If we are looking to go ahead and remove a lot of the traditional legacy systems that we have the buy needs to be a little bit more consistent, we need something like a stable coin to come into play and benefit us in that system. For example, USD Coin that is backed by the U.S. Dollar. So now backing up again to the Defi components that we need for the decentralized infrastructure, we have an Ethereum network ready to go, we have a stable coin, and now we need decentralized financial services.

We need something competitive with the traditional legacy system and the services that they bring to the table. We need something that will allow us to come in and actually start moving our funds around, trading or swapping out in a decentralized way or something like a "Dex" which stands for decentralized exchange. You don't need to have any accounts for you to sign in and no ID verification, it is completely autonomous and free for everybody to come in and utilize it.

This provides a service where the Defi space allows you to come in and trade in a decentralized manner without having any KYC, or to be banned by any government because no government can ban a decentralize exchange. Keep that in mind. So there are little coins and a myriad of projects on decentralized exchanges, but no government could come in and decide to shut it down. There is no owner, no CEO, just a bunch of coders that work on it, It's an open source that anybody can come in and work on. This decentralized space is growing and wide open for people to come in and build on it.

We also need decentralized money market, we also need things that allow you to come in and connect with borrowers and lenders, looking at a bank for instance, they allows you to come in and then connect you to lenders, right? You want to come in and borrow something. The bank says hey, we want to lend you this but do you qualify for us to lend you something? They won't allow you to be the lender, they just allow you to be the borrower, the borrower In decentralized finance, the defi system, you can be either or you can be the lender or the borrower and you're incentivized to vote, right so here's the deal. Let's say you go to a project like compound, which is one of the OG's in the defi space. If you go to compound and you decide that you want to borrow on your compound, you will have to deposit a certain amount of your compound in there, and you say: I want to get a certain amount of Ethereum back. So you put 10,000 compound, and they let you borrow $5,000 worth of Ethereum. Now you have a collateralized loan, right, you put in some you got some back, and once you pay back your $5,000 worth of Ethereum, you'll get your 10,000 compound back. Now, let's say you went out and purchased Bitcoin and it just started going up, or you are just killed it on Ethereum and you decide to run it up and the price goes up. Now essentially what you've just done is you've went ahead, gotten the loan right? You borrowed some money from the compound network or compound project. Now, if it is doubled in price, you're still only on the hook for $5,000 worth of Ethereum.

So essentially, you borrowed, got a free gain and had to pay back what you borrowed. This has happened multiple times, and for a lot of people in the Defi space, when the prices were going up, People were going on products like compound projects, finance projects, the curve projects and balancer. All of these money market projects. They were coming in and borrowing. Now you have lenders that come in and say hey, I have 10k and I want to lend out a certain amount of my Ethereum, right on this project. We want to come in and borrow it and I want to earn a substantial amount as they paid back. So now over time, you'll gain interest.

We are providing that liquidity and being a lender on the platform, so it's this great symbiotic relationship with being able to come in and say, You know what, I want to be my own bank, I want to be the lender or I want to be the borrower, and I have all these incentivizing applications that works with this kind of an asset. Decentralized finance can go leaps and bounds ahead of the traditional system, because we have all of these things that allow people who may have never had a bank account or anything considered to get to be banked by certain banks, they can come in and participate and be fine without having any kind of KYC like I said before, they do not have to come in and verify that they live in a certain area to have a certain amount of income.

This system is open to everyone as long as you have the collateral to put into the market. And I have to say to borrow against your cryptocurrency collateral, it is the autonomous management of the loan term. So there's nobody coming in to decide if you are qualified or not. It is all based on smart contracts where nobody can be denied. If you've ever tried to start a small business, and you went to apply for a loan and they told you no, that goes away with decentralized finance. This is why something like this is so important because there are just places in the world where discrimination just runs rapidly. Defi brings real solutions to real world problems.

This is a real thing that happens to a lot of people all over the globe, not just in the US.

FOURTH QUARTER

FREE GAME

CONTROL YOUR MENTAL SPACE

IGNORANCE OF THE LAW IS NO EXCUSE

The seven hermetic principles upon which the entire hermetic philosophy is based, are as follows:

Number one, the principle of mentalism, "the all is mind," and the universe is mental. This law in and of itself, really is the basis of all we do here. What we do is, we use our mind to bring about change in our reality. The principle embodies the truth that all is mind. It explains that the "all," which is substantial reality, underlining all the outward manifestations in appearances, is spirit, which in itself is unknowable, and undefinable, but it may be considered and thought of as a universal infinite living mind. It also explains that all the phenomenal world or universe is simply a mental creation of the "all" subject to the laws of created things, and that the universe as a whole, emits parts or units, and has its existence in the mind of the "all" in whose mind we move and have our beat.

I found the most practical implementation of this principle is when you combine it with the second one — the principle of correspondence as above, so below as within so without. If we have determined that the all is mind, then we know that the above should mirror the below, and vice versa.

That also means that our own personal small mind is similar to that of the all, the "all" mind — the divine mind, if you will. This means that if all is created in the divine mind, we can create our own reflection of the "all" — a more personal source. Now that we know that we can create with our mind, the first thing you should do is take good care of your thoughts, as your mind is built upon thoughts. Now, if you're inexperienced, if you've never meditated before, if you're new to all of this, it might seem like you do not control your thoughts, and they simply appear. And in a way, that is true. They might be, but it is up to you to accept their truth. So, just as you are not accepting negative thoughts - thoughts that do not suit your purpose - likewise, you want to purposefully and deliberately accept good thoughts that do work for you. Of course, another thing you can start doing once you've gained more control of your thoughts is to start conjuring your own thoughts out of nowhere. One way to do this is through affirmations and subliminal messaging.

Number two, the principle of correspondence. The principle embodies the truth, that there is always a correspondence between the laws and phenomena of the various planes of being in life. The old hermetic axiom ran in these words: as above, so below, as below so above. The grasping of this principle gives one the means of solving many a dark paradox and hidden secret of nature. There are planes beyond our knowing, but when we apply the principle of correspondence to them, we are able to understand much that would otherwise be unknowable to us. This principle is of universal application and manifestation on the various planes of the material, mental and spiritual universe. It is a universal law. So, the knowledge of the principle of correspondence enables men to reason intelligently from the unknown to the unknown.

Next is the principle of vibration. This principle - which really is at the base of the law of attraction if you study further - embodies the truth that everything is in motion, and everything vibrates. Nothing is at rest. This is a fact, which modern science endorses, and which each new scientific discovery tends to verify. Yet, this hermetic principle was enunciated thousands of years ago by the Masters of ancient Egypt. This principle explains that the differences between manifestations of matter, energy, mind and even spirit result largely from varying rates of vibration, from the oil, which is pure spirit, down to the grossest form of matter. All is in vibration. The higher the vibration, the higher the position in the scale. The vibration of the Spirit is at such an infinite rate of intensity and rapidity, that it's practically at rest. There are millions upon millions of varying degrees of vibration. First, it might seem that the principle of mentalism might be the most important one, but a real understanding of the principle of vibration can get you through so much more than simply imagining. Feeling is power, feeling is vibration. Emotions are vibration. When you feel wealthy, you will become wealthy when you tap into the vibration of wealth.

The principle of polarity is yet another principle, which embodies the truth that everything is dual, and everything has two poles. Everything has its pair of opposites, all of which were old hermetic axioms. It explains the old paradoxes that have perplexed so many, which have been stated as follows. Thesis and antithesis are identical in nature, but different in degree; opposites are the same, differing only in degree. All truths are but half-truths. Every truth is half false. There are two sides of everything. It explains that in everything, there are two poles or opposite aspects, and that opposites are really only the two extremes of the same thing, with many varying degrees between them. The principle of polarity explains these paradoxes, and no other principle can supersede it. The same principle operates on the mental plane. When you look at the principle of polarity, you can use it to your advantage. Most people have positive thoughts, so they have a very positive life. But when they have negative thoughts, they have a very negative life. What you should take from this that you should now start to call the shots of your own life. The future effects that you will receive will be because of your current thoughts of today. And likewise, the life you live today is the effect of the negative thoughts or positive thoughts that you have had months, years, or even decades ago. For some people, these thoughts stem from the subconscious messaging that their parents gave them in their childhood. So, it is very important to seize control over your own subconscious mind. When you start to realize that really, nothing is random, and everything has been decided by your own thoughts and mental creations, you'll be more intentional about them.

The next principle, which is principle of rhythm embodies the truth that in everything, there is manifested and measured motion to and fro, a flow in inflow, a swing backward and forward, a pendulum like movement. A tide like ebb and flow, a high tide and low tide between the two poles, which exists in accordance with that of the principle of polarity described a moment ago. There is always an action in the reaction and an advance and a retreat, arising in a sinking. This is the affair of the universe, suns, worlds, men, animals, mind, energy and matter. This law is manifested in the creation and destruction of worlds, in the rise and fall of nations, in the life of all things, and finally, in the mental states of men.

The principle of cause and effect. This principle embodies the fact that there is a cause for every effect and effect from every cause. It explains that everything happens according to law, that nothing ever merely happens and there is no such thing as chance. There are various planes of cause and effect - the higher dominating the lower planes - but still, nothing ever entirely escapes the law. To understand the art and methods of rising above the ordinary plane of cause and effect to a certain degree and by mentally rising to a higher plane, is to become a causer instead of an effect. The masses of people are carried along, obedient to environment, the wills and desires of others stronger than themselves, heredity, suggestion and other outward causes.

The last but not the least principle is the principle of gender. Principle of gender is a very underrated one, but very important because once again, it shows us and gives us a deeper level of understanding of how creation works. It works through the feminine and the masculine. This principle embodies the truth that there is gender manifested in everything; the masculine and feminine principles ever at work. This is true, not only of the physical plane, but of the mental and even spiritual planes on the physical plane. This principle manifests as sex on the higher planes, and there, it takes higher forms, but the principle is ever the same. No creation - physical, mental or spiritual - is possible without this principle, and understanding of its laws will throw light on many a subject that has perplexed the minds of men. The principle of gender works ever in the direction of generation, regeneration and creation. Everything and every person possess the two elements or principles of this great principles within him or her. Every male thing has the female element. Likewise, every female also has the male principle. The feminine is the subconscious mind, while the masculine is the conscious mind. You must impregnate your subconscious mind, which is feminine; it receives everything which draws everything in it. Whatever the subconscious mind sees, hears, or whatever thoughts occur within the mind, it accepts. Therefore, you must be careful what you impregnate your subconscious mind. Also, make sure that with your masculine mind, you give enough power to the impregnation, as power is emotion.

All of these principles are important, as they work together to form one beautiful whole creation. There is no law higher than the law of the universe, yet, we tend to focus on the laws of the land alone. The truth is, laws of the universe will free you mentally and spiritually — something the law of the land cannot and will not do.

CHAKRAS

The seven chakras are the vital centers of spiritual power within the human body through which energy flows freely from one chakra to the next. And these energetic centers help regulate all the internal functions of our bodies, such as boosting the immune system, regulating our emotions and allowing us to connect with elevated consciousness, which is our higher self. The chakras themselves are positioned in a straight-line configuration, starting from the base of the spine to the crown of the head.

Each chakra has its own vibrational frequency which in turn is represented by a particular color. Let's begin at the base of the spine. This first chakra is called the root chakra. This chakra provides us with everything we need to survive and prosper, such as water stability, security and physical energy. When it's not functioning properly, we will feel zero energy. We might also tend to develop problems in our legs or spine.

Now, let's move on to the second chakra. This chakra is called the sacral chakra and it's located just below your navel. The purpose of this chakra is to look after your bladder, kidneys reproductive system and lower abdomen. This chakra deals with the emotional body sensuality and creativity. It is the center of our feelings and sensations, which are the driving force for the enjoyment of our life through the five senses. This chakra not functioning properly develops problems in your bladder and your pelvic area.

The third chakra is called the solar plexus chakra, which is located in your stomach region. This chakra makes sure that your stomach, your liver, intestines and digestive justice system are working properly. The purpose of this chakra is to help us find direction in life. It also allows us to take the actions needed in order to reach our goals. The solar plexus chakra also acts as a line of defense that protects our moral code and integrity, making sure we don't stray too far from our own path and not allow other people's opinions and negative beliefs to influence our state of mind or decision. When your solar plexus chakra is out of balance, you might suffer indigestion, and liver and pancreas problems. You might also have trouble standing up for what you believe in or saying no.

Let's move our attention to the fourth chakra. This chakra is called the heart chakra, which is located in the chest region. Its function is to look after our heart, lungs and circulatory system. Heart chakra keeps our heart open and loving, making it easier for us to express our emotions and allowing us to be more passionate towards others. The heart chakra also acts as a purification system for all the other chakras, thereby cleansing the negative emotions and allowing our entire energy field to remain positive. When there is a blockage in the heart chakra, you may experience difficulty relating to others, excessive jealously, codependence, lack of sympathy and bitterness. Imbalance within this chakra may bring about several health issues such as heart-related problems, lung infections and bronchitis.

The throat chakra, as the name implies, is located in the throat region and looks after the throat, thyroid, neck and jaw. This chakra, essentially helps you find your true authentic voice and assist you in expressing yourself, thereby making it a key component in verbal communication. Behavioral and psychological characteristics associated with this chakra include good sense of timing, realizing your vocation, purpose, a propensity to project ideas into reality. Another function of this chakra is to connect you with the etheric realm, the more subtle realms of spirit and your intuitive abilities. When the throat chakra is blocked, it causes lack of control of one's speech, speaking too much or inappropriately for example, not being able to listen to others, excessive fear of public speaking, inability to keep secrets or your word, and you may even tell lies.

On to the sixth, most commonly referred to as the third eye chakra, which is located in the center of the forehead, between and above the eyebrows. This chakra looks after the brain neurological system, eyes, ears and nose. It also has the ability to unlock the power of the mind, and thus, help teach us how to heal ourselves, and change our life on the willpower. The third eye chakra can give us vision, intuition, perception of subtle dimensions and movements of energy. It connects us to wisdom, insight, and can unlock psychic abilities related to clairvoyance. An imbalance with the third eye chakra can cause lack of clarity, rejection of the spiritual, feeling stuck and unable to see past our problems in order to find a solution. It can cause health problems associated with the brain such as blurry vision, insomnia, sinus issues and nausea.

The final of the seven-chakra system is called the crown chakra. This chakra is located at the top of the head. Its function is to look after your upper brain and nervous system. The Crown Chakra gives us access to higher states of awareness that allows us to access the universal consciousness, and will help to awaken you to the highest truth that you are an infinite being inside a temporary human body. People who suffer from imbalanced Crown Chakra experience close-mindedness, and may also develop neurological disorders, Alzheimer's, insomnia and depression. You may also experience recurring headaches and migraines. As you can see, the chakras play a very important role in our well-being, and that's why it's very important to make sure that they are working properly. Otherwise, our bodies will be out of balance, congested with negativity and stress, that causes blockages in these centers. When the internal chakra system is not working properly, the mind and body begin to malfunction.

POWER WITHIN

Semen retention - some of you might know it as nofap - is generally a practice of not engaging in any form of sexual stimulation or ejaculation whether through pornography, casual sexual intercourse or masturbation. The main purpose of semen retention is to revert our brains' inclination towards the pursuit of more and more pleasure. And in this case, it is specifically for those individuals who are addicted to porn and excessive masturbation. It is understandable that we as men have a great and natural urge to procreate, and if those tendencies and urges go unfulfilled, we find a way to release those urges through some other form of conduct.

Unfortunately, many men go about doing this the wrong way. Instead of transferring this energy into more constructive endeavors, we waste it away with impulsive and mindless acts such as watching porn and self-ejaculating. A man's semen is his life force and what distinguishes him from others of his kind.

When you empty your tank of life of force or semen, it will render you defenseless and inevitably more vulnerable to predators. Not to mention, it actually takes a long time to produce semen. Think about the fact that semen is powerful enough to produce a new life and contains enough essential nutrients to nourish and actually grow another human life. Wasting away your semen on digital porn instead of purposeful procreation is a total disregard for the value of the power inside you. Your semen, when not ejaculated, is left to mature and be reabsorbed through your body and blood stream, nourishing it with its nutrient-dense contents and bringing biological benefits of both mental and physical nature.

When you ejaculate, it makes you feel like you've made it or reached a significant goal which is a false signal to your brain and body to relax. Men have an inherent desire to procreate and attract women with our looks, finance and status. It takes time to actually meet and develop chemistry for real sex, but porn and masturbation offer unrealistic instant gratification that is short lived. Frequent ejaculation causes you to be depleted of your life force and natural nutrients, and this in turn causes low energy, lack of motivation, foggy mind and depression.

One of the things to be ready for when you start to retain your semen is clarity of mind — your mind will just be clear. Your train of thoughts will be more organized, and you'll be more assertive. The second one is physical strength. You will experience more strength, energy, and higher performance. Thirdly, determination and focus. Imagine being locked into the motion of your work or whatever - whether it is writing a script, or designing a presentation - to the point where you just lose all sense of time until you're completely done with your work. Being laser locked on your work or whatever you're doing is great. The fourth — directness. The offspring of having laser-guided focus is the demeanor of being direct with everything with no hesitation or sugar coating. The fifth and most important benefit and also a product of all the other benefits is confidence. Confidence is something that you acquire over time through success and failure. Being able to exercise self-control over your sexual urges and seeing the benefits you were missing is a great success. Being more confident automatically increases your attraction. What you do with the benefits of semen retention is what will make you more valuable as a man. Semen retention is not a cure or answer to your problems, but a tool to be used to your advantage in building yourself spiritually, mentally, financially, physically and intellectually. From then on, you must begin to take action.

TOXIC SOCIAL MEDIA USAGE

I know a lot of people like weed, but I don't find that it is very good for productivity. I like to get things done; I like to be useful. And one of the hardest things to do with weed is, be useful. Even more so, when you're stuck on social media, scrolling all day and night.

With social media sites being used by 1/3 of the entire world, they clearly have a major influence on society. But what about our bodies? Social media and the internet are affecting your brain right now. Can't log off? Surprisingly, 5-10% of Internet users are actually unable to control how much time they spend online. But it's a psychological addiction as opposed to a substance addiction. Brain scans of these people actually show with similar impairment of regions that those with drug dependence have. Specifically, there's a clear degradation of the white matter in the regions that control emotional processing attention and decision making. Because social media provides immediate rewards, with very little effort required, your brain begins to rewire itself, making you desire these stimulations, and then you'll begin to create more of this neurological excitement after each interaction. Sounds a little like a drug, right? We also see a shift when looking at multitasking. You might think that those who use social media or constantly switch between work and websites are better at multitasking, but studies have found that when comparing heavy media users to others, they perform much worse during task switching tests. Increased multitasking online reduces your brain's ability to filter out interferences and can even make it harder for your brain to commit information to memory like when your phone is in the middle of productive work, or even buzz.

Phantom vibration syndrome is a relatively new psychological phenomenon where you think your phone is going off, but it isn't. In one study, 89% of test subjects that they experienced this at least once every two weeks. It would seem that our brains now perceive an itch as an actual vibration from our funnel. As crazy as it seems, technology has begun to rewire our nervous systems, and our brains are being triggered in a way they never have before in history.

Social media also triggers the release of dopamine effect. Using MRI scans, the scientists have found that the reward centers in people's brains are much more active when they're talking about their own views as opposed to listening to others. Not so surprising. We all are talking about ourselves, but it turns out that well 30 to 40% of face-to-face conversations involve communicating our own experiences, and around 80% of social media communication is self-involved. And the same part of your brain related to orgasms, motivation and love are stimulated by your social media use and even more so, when you know you have an audience, your body is physiologically rewarding you for talking about yourself online, but it's not also self-involved. In fact, studies on relationships have found that partners tend to like each other more if they meet for the first time online rather than with a face-to-face interaction. Whether it's because people are more anonymous or perhaps clearer about their future goals, there's a statistical increase in successful partnerships that started online. So, while the Internet has changed our verbal communication with increased physical separation, perhaps the ones that matter the most end up even closer. You need time to get things done. A distraction is a subtraction. Stop robbing your own success.

PHYSICAL FITNESS

Physical training can help build mental fortitude. Every man must participate in some form of physical training in their lives in order to consistently serve that purpose. The human body was conceived mainly for survival. Its purpose is to help us survive, whether it involves facing threatening circumstances, or even circumstances that are ever so slightly detrimental to our own well-being. It is in its nature to help us survive, and we can't change anything about that. Unfortunately, many people still disregard their own body as a disposable suit of armor, or just a host for them to exploit, instead of treating it like the prize that it is. They just discreetly ignore and destroy them over time, or they just leave them to rot and completely waste the profound potential that it can provide. Your body is the greatest, most effective and most efficient, adaptive machine in this world. It always has the capability and the capacity to adapt, withstand, tolerate and overcome every stimulus that your body is physically exposed to. You will naturally and innately find possible ways to control them to the extent that, once you find yourself in a place where the weather is cold and expose your body to it, your body will internally reconfigure itself to eventually help you be at ease with that condition. This feature is what is widely defined as the fight or flight mode, where our body naturally perceives circumstances as harmful detrimental by threatening, and will enable us to face the challenge, threat or suffering, and go into full survival mode. A simple example would be people who can take spicy foods. People who have a tolerance to those spices certainly didn't start off doing it. It came from tolerance, by exposing their physical sensitivities to the stimulus for a very, very long time; thus, the body made adjustments to tolerate and overcome the burning taste. Exactly the same principle applies to physical training, whether you're lifting weights doing boxing, wrestling, or any form of martial arts. Your body is slowly but surely making adaptations to suit itself around and within those situations. The more you expose yourself to weight-lifting, your muscles will get bigger, fat will drop, and your bones will get denser. Similarly, the more you expose yourself to other sports of your choice, you'll jump higher, run faster, swim swifter and hold your breath longer. Your body is capable of amazing feats. And yes, some of you might say some people have literally good genetics that have served them well in physical training. While I agree with that, it can also be a silly pitiful excuse not to build your body to a great potential for it to serve you. Well, your body wants to serve you and wants to protect you. And to do that, you must expose them to situations and circumstances that allow them to grow and fine-tune itself to serve you better. Your body will only grow and serve you certainly well when you put it to the test, keep testing its limits and give it what it needs to achieve growth. Let's talk about the things that are destroying your body instead of allowing it to grow. And yes, I'm talking about all the things in this day and age that have become a huge part of the cultural norms. They include excessive smoking, drug usage, processed foods, sugar, alcohol and the one almost everybody suffers from today — the lack of sleep.

The more you drink alcohol, your body develops tolerance. The more you smoke, your body develops tolerance to nicotine. But in those endeavors, they don't give what the body needs to grow, which is proper and healthy nutrition. This tolerance leads to addiction; you don't exactly seek tolerance from them, but the feeling they provide makes you seek more of them, and that's how your tolerance level increases.

Feed your body nutrient dense, organic, natural and healthy foods that contain the essential macro and micro nutrients. Keep your body hydrated by shooting for a gallon of water daily and getting good quality sleep to recover. Your body is the engine, and the things it requires to perform are the fuel sources.

Just like a car, if you feed the engine contaminated fuel, used lubricants and dirty water, how do you expect it to perform as well as it should? Good physical training routines are great to make your body get to its greatest potential. And your sources of fuel for your body do not only affect you physically, but affect you mentally as well. Your mood, demeanor and energy will tremendously influence how your mind operates cognitively. There's an old saying that you are what you do and you are what you eat, and that can never be truer. That is why I'm preaching this to you. The Healthy Body will always translate to a healthy mind. When speaking about mentality, let's discuss on how physical training can help build a strong and dependable mental fortitude. You see, the byproduct that comes from what you decide to go through physically translate tremendously well to what you can go through mentally, because the narrative of facing challenges and adversities is always the same for everyone for everything.

Physical training is the first and simplest form or level of facing adversity. You can almost call it one of the main analogies to be used in facing adversity. I faced this adversity when I first got into prison; I was unable to do pull-ups but eventually, I overcame it, and now, I'm able to do many sets of pull-ups. Lifting heavy weights and getting physically strong are not easy tasks. To accomplish anything rewarding never comes easy. First, you want to use those weights that you're lifting. And it was grueling and gradual process to allow your body to morph into its desired state to get you comfortable with those weights. And then when you are comfortable, you progress into heavier weights and bigger adversities to face. To suffer first and then to reap the rewards after is amazing. Physical training teaches you the genesis of discipline, consistency, commitment, persistence and sacrifice, and the rewards that you report will cause you to trust those principles, and to be strongly planted and embedded within the mentality, which then can be applied to other meaningful and purposeful activities in your life such as business, education, projects and your relationships. The state of the body is important to your state of mind as well. Physical training should be done for your health and well-being. You should always be your own mental point of focus in your life by committing yourself to consistent physical training. It exudes a great level of self-respect, integrity and dignity

You always have time, it's just a matter of priorities.

PLANT-BASED LIFESTYLE

Being in prison, I realized how the prison, medical, and pharmaceutical systems all work together to produce revenue and further their agendas. Do you know that if you didn't take the COVID vaccine in prison, these people actually threatened that you wouldn't be able to parole out or get accepted into transitional centers? The remedies that are provided in prison for chronic care conditions are designed to have you take the medication that they provide. For example, my LDL cholesterol came back in the high range after a general blood test, but everything else was fine. HDL was good, as well as my blood pressure, lungs and heart. With no mention of diet, immediately, I was prescribed statins that lowered my cholesterol within weeks, but they came with terrible side effects, so I stopped taking them.

A few months later, blood work showed that my cholesterol had risen back up since I stopped the meds, so the doctor recommended a different statin for me to test out. I requested an herbal remedy, but he said that was the last course of action in the event that the statins didn't work. Within two weeks of taking the statins, I experienced the same side effects as before, combined with psychological issues like anxiety and depression. I stopped taking them and then requested an advanced lipid profile. In response, they switched my doctor to one with a more aggressive demeanor, who went on and on, trying to convince me of the danger I was in with high cholesterol, and how they couldn't do advanced lipid screening or provide alternative medicine to the statins. By the way, statins are a medication for cholesterol that you have to take for the rest of your life. I started to look into the plant-based diet and this is what I found:

People who have adopted a whole food plant-based diet have actually been able to not just control or manage their eating habits, but also, reverse their chronic illness while coming off their medications.

For most people, the biggest surprise is that they actually get well. You know, in medicine, if you have high blood pressure, diabetes, obesity, autoimmune diseases, lymphoma, etc., you'd often be told that you can't get well, or that you'd be sick the rest of your life. But with this approach, the shocking thing is, the body is able to do what it does best — heal itself.

It lowers the weight and cholesterol, and also controls blood pressure. Doctors have had patients go off their insulin and go off their blood pressure medications. There have been cases where diabetes has been completely reversed, and where high blood sugar level have gone back to normal, without insulin, merely because the people involved changed what they put at the end of their fork. It's very inspiring to see the bloat leave their faces, and the beautiful jaw lines appear.

For some, the interesting change was, their acne clearing up, better sleep, waking up alert in the morning and not falling asleep in the middle of the afternoon. People who used to go get a cup of coffee at two o'clock, and now, are more energetic.

Yes, the weight loss and yes, the blood sugars drop. The blood pressure and the cholesterol levels get better. Other people come in and they say things like their joints feel better. Suddenly, those that couldn't open a jar of spaghetti three weeks ago, are now able to do it now.

When they first got these symptoms, they wondered, "Is this just a side effect of the diet that no one ever told us about?" So, they read up on those little surprises, and realized that that was where their skin cleared up, and their psoriasis is gone. Just this amazing, holistic benefits to the entire body.

A lot of people see that they have improved digestion. So, whether it's gas, bloating, constipation, abdominal pain — all those digestive problems seem to relieve themselves. And people also become a lot more active. You get a lot of energy, and then you just feel like you don't know what you're supposed to do with this energy, and then you start working out and having a good time.

What is also kind of unexpected is that minor ailments can be improved; for example, things like allergies. A lot of people blame the allergies on their cat or their pollen in the in the air from the trees. As a matter of fact, those things might be a trigger, but when you remove the inflammatory substances from what you're eating, then you actually are able to tolerate all of those other environmental triggers a lot better. So, I've seen people who no longer have to take allergy medicines every day, once they eliminate animal foods. A little bit more unusual thing is, people get better from their skin allergies and their chronic sinus congestion.

Usual stuff also happen, like treatment of diabetes and heart disease, and the cholesterol lowers. Common testimonies include better sleep, more energy, reversal of chronic issues they've had for years, etc. it could be a chronic ache or pain, a skin issue, or perhaps a belly or GI issue. There are people who have had prostatitis or inflammation of the prostate for years, and have done all the regular therapies; this condition which is quite debilitating, went away after adopting a plant-based diet. People with cystitis inflamed bladder have also affirmed that they were healed after this. No, I can't unequivocally prove that that's from the diet, but that's the only thing that changed. Doctor's also have many patients who have been healed of their erectile dysfunction. It's improved sexual function, not just for men, but women as well.

People notice right off the bat that they have more energy. It certainly boosts the energy. Plant-based foods have been found to activate our MAP kinase, which is an energy center; hence, it definitely boosts up our energy levels. Energy levels increase exponentially while on this diet. And this is a complete surprise to them that they have energy in your pocket they have and they're able to use it in all sorts of ways extra activities to be more romantic with their partner, and be able to do all the kinds of things that they would usually make excuses for. The most common excuse is that they're too tired. Your sex life improves dramatically because it involves blood flow. Think about it. I mean, what's impotence? It's blood. Lack of blood flow to the penis. So, instead of taking Viagra, all you have to do is eat kale, and then you'll have the same blood flow as females. When you're eating a diet full of antioxidants and micronutrients, you have increased blood flow everywhere. Another benefit that is really unexpected is that diet with erectile dysfunction or who might just occasionally have a problem getting it up; they will often find that that is completely no longer a problem. And the reason for that is, there's plaque in the arteries from a standard process involved in producing animal foods, and we tend to think that it's only related to the heart. Well, as a matter of fact, smaller arteries are affected first. So, the penile arteries get affected and they have plaque too. When that happens, blood flow declines.

Competitive athletes report how by simply changing their diet, their time for running a mile goes down. They're able to work out more intensely and more quickly, and there's plenty of pathophysiologic rationale to back that up. If they have a problem with pooping on a regular basis, their constipation is improved. And the reason for that is that the average person eating up standard-processed diet that might include 10 to 15 grams of fiber a day. The recommendation is to get 25 to 30 grams of fiber a day, but a plant-based eaters can get 60 to 100 grams of fiber a day.

When you finally start eating whole plant foods, you get tons of fiber that give amazing benefits. I think people are surprised at the level of happiness. It seems like I'm nicer; people have told me that I feel like I'm being a nicer person. Well, when you don't feel terrible, you can be a lot nicer. Not only did I lose weight, my cholesterol plummeted, my sleep apnea went away, and the irregular heart rhythm went away as well. Even more amazing were the effects on my mood and my productivity at work and my general energy levels. My allergies went away, which I never, never expected — I never even thought about that. I had had lifelong seasonal allergies, for which I had to take drugs and nasal sprays. The first average season after my plant-based diet, they went away. I think we don't talk about the profound impact the American diet has, not only on our health directly, but the inflammation; it is highly inflammatory, and contributes to many of these diseases, allergies, asthma and even many chronic autoimmune diseases. When you get rid of those sugar highs and lows, you no longer need a soda candy bar in the morning or three in the afternoon to sustain yourself at work. Your productivity level goes up, and this gives you more time to exercise at the end of the day. The obesity melts away, the arteries open up and the high blood pressure goes down. The joints stop hurting, then the skin clears up and the bowel starts working. These things are turned around by this. We mentioned diabetes. We mentioned hypertension. We mentioned strokes. We mentioned vascular dementia, ulcerative colitis, Crohn's disease, rheumatoid arthritis, lupus, multiple sclerosis, allergies, and the list goes on. These conditions were absolutely stopped and reversed with plant-based diet. I think it'll be a good idea to become Vegan or start transitioning to a more plant-based meals.

OVERTIME

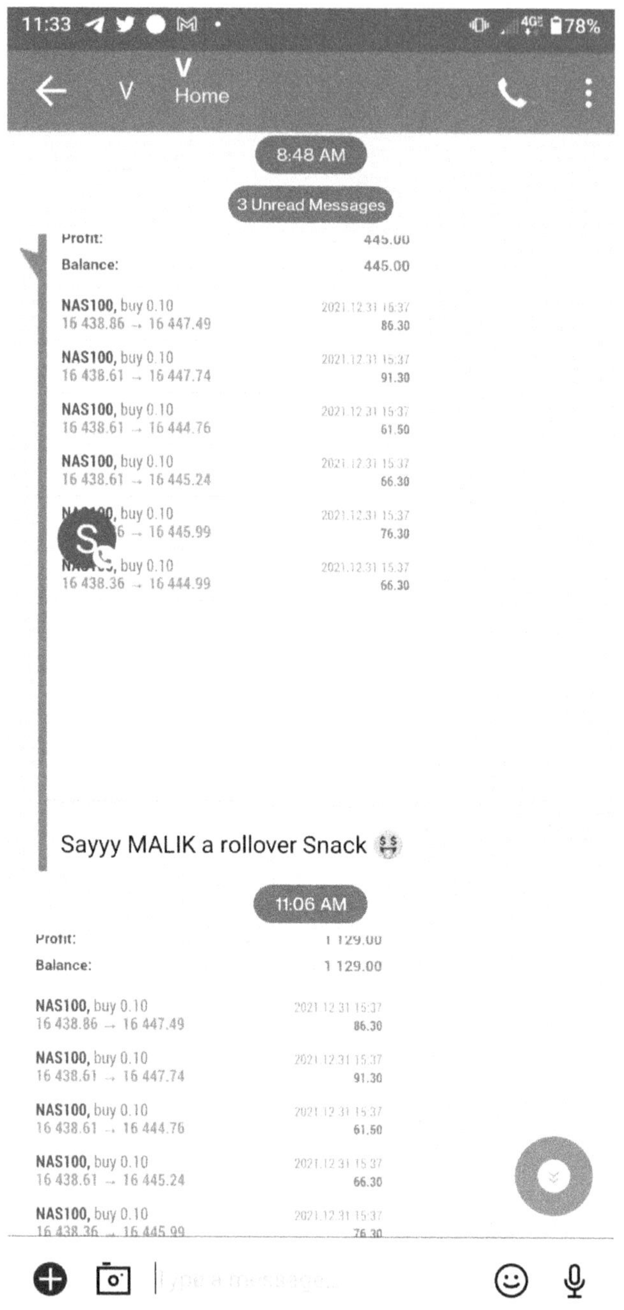
11:33
78%
V
V
Home
8:48 AM
3 Unread Messages
Profit: 445.00
Balance: 445.00
NAS100, buy 0.10
16 438.86 → 16 447.49
2021.12.31 15:37
86.30
NAS100, buy 0.10
16 438.61 → 16 447.74
2021.12.31 15:37
91.30
NAS100, buy 0.10
16 438.61 → 16 444.76
2021.12.31 15:37
61.50
NAS100, buy 0.10
16 438.61 → 16 445.24
2021.12.31 15:37
66.30
, buy 0.10
6 → 16 445.99
2021.12.31 15:37
76.30
, buy 0.10
16 438.36 → 16 444.99
2021.12.31 15:37
66.30
Sayyy MALIK a rollover Snack
11:06 AM
Profit: 1 129.00
Balance: 1 129.00
NAS100, buy 0.10
16 438.86 → 16 447.49
2021.12.31 15:37
86.30
NAS100, buy 0.10
16 438.61 → 16 447.74
2021.12.31 15:37
91.30
NAS100, buy 0.10
16 438.61 → 16 444.76
2021.12.31 15:37
61.50
NAS100, buy 0.10
16 438.61 → 16 445.24
2021.12.31 15:37
66.30
NAS100, buy 0.10
16 438.36 → 16 445.99
2021.12.31 15:37
76.30

FREE GAME

FIND YOUR LEGIT LANE & STAY OUT THE WAY

REPLACE YOUR PRISON WITH EIN

Your EIN is your employer identification number, which is also known as your federal tax ID number. It is a nine-digit number that the IRS created to separate businesses from each other, so that's very similar. This is actually pretty much the same thing as a social security number for your business. And the reasons you will want to get an EIN number is, one, you plan on having employees. So, if you are a single member LLC, or a sole proprietor, you might not need one, but I'll give reasons why people who have a single member LLC and sole proprietor decide to get one. One of the main reasons is to separate your finances. So, you're going to want to separate your business accounts from your personal accounts, and you will do that with your EIN number. So, with your EIN number, you'll be able to open up a business checking account, and they'll use that to keep your finances separate from your personal account. The second reason businesses apply for their EIN number is to establish business credit. That way, when you're applying for loans for your business, it won't be in your personal name; instead, it'll be your business name, and you won't require your social security number. Any time you're applying for it, you can long on to irs.gov. A lot of people go through

LegalZoom or someone else that charges them a couple $100s to apply for something that's free. You want to pay close attention to this because it could save you a couple $100s.

Now, before you get your EIN number, there are a few things you need to know because some of us think that once we get our EIN number, we can just go start applying for credit, which is true for the most part, but you need to make sure that you also have a very clear understanding of the things that need to be set in place before you do. So, one, make sure you have your name, and make sure it's catchy. Make sure it's not too long, and make sure it's universal. Domain. There are several places that you guys can purchase a domain from, just make sure yours is available. That way, if you want to be dot com, you don't have to choose to be dotnet because someone else has that website. Also, this is a great time for you guys to start building on your website because they take time. Even if you're tech savvy, it still takes a little time if you want to have a really nice website. So, pay for your domain, start building your website, look around, see what they cost and see who can do it for you. Look at other people's work as well. Number three, professional phone number and fax number. We'll make sure we have a professional phone number and fax number. We are not putting down a house, a home number or a cell phone number; it is going to be professional. For a professional email address, no Gmail, or Yahoo; strictly professional. For instance, my company is Slick Chisel Fitness, and my email is support@slickchiselfit.com. You're going to need a professional email address, so make sure you get that all right. If you don't have a physical address, get a virtual address. We're not using home addresses and we're not using P.O.

boxes or anything of the sort. Get a virtual office before you get your EIN number. Be sure to decide whether you want to be a LLC, sole proprietor, S Corp, or C Corp. Before you make a decision, make a lot of research. Make sure you find out what's best for your business and choose wisely.

After you get your EIN number, you are to register with the Secretary of State. You have already established your LLC. But when you go to register with the Secretary of State, if you do not plan on attaching LLC to your business name when you make your business cards, flyers, or every time you fill out some paperwork- don't attach LLC to your business name when you register. Don't put that behind your name when you register. Everything has to be the exact same with the register when you register with the Secretary of State, just like when you fill out any type of business application for business financing or even a vendor credit, okay? So, everything must be the same. If you're filling out vendor credit and you have LLC behind your name, what will you register with the Secretary of State? If you don't have it behind your name when you're building your business credit, you might look like a totally different business and get denied. So, everything needs to look the same because there are businesses that have the similar names. When you are applying for vendor credit, you also must make sure you are listed, or you're at risk of getting denied. Make sure you get listed; you can get listed with 411, as they do it for free. And there are several other places that you can get listed, so, do it. Make sure you do those five steps before you even get your EIN number, and definitely before you register with the Secretary of State.

Everything that's on your paperwork with the Secretary of State should match everything that's on your paperwork when you are applying for any type of business credit. And remember, if you don't, you can go back and change it with the Secretary of State because addresses do change. You might have a virtual office now and then you go get your storefront, and that would mean that the address would change. You can change it with the Secretary of State. Make sure when anything changes, you change it with the Secretary of State. However, it will cost you to change your details depending on what you're changing, and it also depends on what state you're in.

CREDIT IS KING

I started worked on my credit while in prison - a couple of years before my release - by getting a credit card in my name and using it to make commissary and prison package purchases for myself. Then I would take the money I made off contraband to pay my credit card down each month. Once I got out, my credit score was a 740, and Capital One gave me a credit card with $7500 credit limit within weeks of me being home from prison. I was able to get an auto loan from the bank with no down payment and all. I even got a personal loan from the bank as well. In my opinion guys, having great credit is essential to building wealth. And the reason I believe it's essential to building wealth is because it gives you access to money; money that you can then leverage to make more money.

There are five categories that make up your credit score, and I'll explain each. Timely payments make up 35% of your credit score. Credit utilization makes up 30% of your credit score. Length of payment history makes up 15% of your credit score. Number of trade lines makes up 10% of your credit score and lastly, hard inquiries make up 10% of your credit score. Now that we know the five categories that make up the credit score, let's talk about some things you should know about your credit report. You need to be able to access your credit score, and you can do that through annual credit report.com which is a federal government sanctioned platform for people like you and I to be able to go and retrieve our credit report at no cost.

Once you retrieve your credit report, then you need to see what's on your credit report. You need to make sure the things that are on your credit report are accurate. If they're not accurate, then my recommendation is, when in doubt, dispute the items on that credit report. Now, let's move on to the 10 tips to boost your credit score. The first tip to boost your credit score is through secured credit cards or secured loans. The way that would work is you would go into your local bank or a credit union, or you would apply online and you would apply for a secured credit card. But first, they'll ask you how much you want to apply for. Let's say you say $500. What you want to do then is take $500 and secure that card as collateral. The reason you want to do that is because if you're new to credit, or you had a bad experience with credit and your score is low, you want to establish new credit. One way to do that is through the secured credit card or a secured loan that will show up as a new trade line. You will start utilizing that card and then paying it off each month, and that's going to be a positive trade line on your credit report in turn, boosting your credit score immediately.

The second way to boost your credit score is becoming an authorized user. You will pick someone who has great credit and they would add you to one of their credit cards. Let's say they had a credit card with a five-year history rate repayment history. Great trade line. Great utilization. Then they would add you as a user to that card, and now you have a trade line with five years' worth of great repayment history and five years of great credit utilization, which in turn will boost your credit score.

The third way to boost your credit score is by asking for credit card increases. Credit utilization is 30% of your credit score. If you ask for an increase from 500 to $1,000 and you were approved for it, now, you have $1,000 credit limit, and your balance is $250, which represents a 25% credit utilization which will boost your score because you're under the 30% credit utilization.

The fourth way to boost your credit score is by not opening new accounts. Here's an example. If I have five trade lines, and all of my trade lines are mediocre trade lines, some of them are paid on time. For some of them I don't pay on time, my credit utilization is higher than 30%. And it's not a good idea for you to be opening new accounts. In this case, I would recommend that you be focused on the current accounts, get the utilization under 30% and make sure you correct your late payments. So, delay opening new accounts until you take care of that current account, and that should boost your credit score.

The fifth way to boost your credit score is to get current on any trade lines that are past due, and make multiple payments throughout the month. So, let's say I have a $200 minimum payment that's due. Instead of me paying all of that $200 on the due date, I would pay it 15 days before the due date, and then I would make a second payment right before the due date. So, now, I'm making two payments before my due date by making those multiple payments; that shows you have the capacity and the willingness to repay, and that will in turn boost your credit score.

The sixth way to boost your credit score is by not making sudden large purchases. If historically, my purchases on my credit cards are below $500, and all of a sudden make a $2,000 purchase, that could affect my credit score. It could actually affect it negatively, so, try to be consistent with your purchases.

The seventh way to boost your credit score is by paying down recent collection accounts. Your credit bureau obviously has recent activity and older activity. The more recent activity is really what the main part of your credit score is dependent on; older activities are also calculated, but they're less important. So, if you have collection accounts that are less than 12 months old, I would ask you to consider paying those off. Now, before you pay off any of those, you are to make sure you connect with the creditor and get a letter from them, stating that if you pay them, they're going to completely remove that negative item from your credit report. If they're not willing to remove that negative item, then don't pay it off. Because a collection account is a collection account whether it's a zero balance or a $5,000 balance, it still is weighted the same. So, the only way I would agree to pay them is if they agree to remove that collection account from my credit report. If you can get them to do that, that will boost your credit score.

The eighth way to boost your credit score is to avoid carrying balances on your credit card. Now I'm not saying, don't use the credit card, because if you don't use it and your credit card company closes the credit card, it will decrease your credit score. What I'm saying is, use the cards, but pay them off in full every single month. If you do that, that will certainly boost your credit score.

The ninth way to boost your credit score is to avoid introductory rates. These credit card companies are in business to make money, even if it may be a zero-interest credit card offer, you still have to make some type of minimum payment on it, right? If you are late on that minimum payment, your zero-interest rate is going to be gone. They're going to increase your interest rate to whatever the maximum they can increase it to because you were late. And the sad part about it is, you've already transferred the balance and you got to be at 20, 25 or even 30% interest rate. So, stay away from introductory offers if you can if you do that, so you can have an opportunity to boost your credit score. The tenth and final tip to boost your credit score is by consolidating your debt. The reason you would consolidate the debt is, it takes you from multiple units to one page. The only way I would consider consolidating that is through a credit union. The credit unions are typically not for profit, so, they're owned by the members of the credit union people like you and me; this means that they have a vested interest in taking care of people and trying to do the best thing for them with respect to their banking needs. Go to your local credit union, sit down with them. Talk to them about consolidating some debt that you'd like to consolidate into a loan. They're going to give you a fair interest rate and you got to be able to at that point, pay off all of those credit cards or installment loans to that consolidation loan. In return, you will be able to boost your credit score by having that one payment you can be able to make every month and not be late because of multiple payments that you likely cannot pay every month. Credit is King.

DIGITAL ENTREPRENEURSHIP

E-commerce stands for electronic commerce. All it is, is selling a product or service online. E-commerce has expanded exponentially in recent years and will only continue to do so. And the more it continues, the more it will continue. Small and medium-sized businesses all the way through to large corporations, and even independent freelances have benefited from e-commerce. Products and services are now so easy to discover and purchase at any hour of any day from almost anywhere in the world. The possibility to scale in this day and age is like no other. E-commerce is the fastest-growing retail market, so why wouldn't you want to be a part of that? There are loads of benefits to hopping on the e-commerce bandwagon. With e-commerce being electronic, you have a global market. This multiplies your target audience exponentially. You also choose who your customers are and define how to target them. With your store being online, you're essentially open 24/7, 365 days a year. There is no need to flip that sign on your front door that states open on one side and closed on the other. Customers can purchase your goods all day, any day. You also have the ability to work from anywhere in the world, provided that you have an internet connection. Another great perk is, you're also going to require a lower investment and incur reduced costs compared to a physical store.

So, who can open an e-commerce store? Anyone really, provided that they have the few essentials to get started. These essentials include a product or service to sell, a place to sell them, a means to process payments, and a marketing strategy to attract customers. Let's discuss each of these a little further. So, right off the bat, you're going to need a product or service to sell. You can either make something yourself, or you can source it from somewhere else. Some things you want to keep in mind are those who you want to sell your product or service to, and the product or service you want to sell; you want something unique. You don't want to sell something that every other Tom, Dick and Harry is selling. What's the point? It would mean more competition and less chances of sales.

Also, try to think of a product or service that solves someone's problem. No one likes having problems, so, it is important for you to have something that can solve enough people's problems. Another point to consider is the cost of your goods and your selling price. You want to price your products at a low enough rate, so that you can compete with similar products on the market. However, you don't want to price yourself too low that you don't make a sufficient profit to keep operating, and at the same time, you don't want to price yourself too high, otherwise, no one will purchase your products. And we don't want that.

Next, you'll need to figure out where you will be selling your goods. The nature of e-commerce is selling online, so, you're not going to be looking for a brick-and-mortar location or physical storefront; instead, you'll need a website or an e-commerce platform to sell your products. You can either build your own website or use a CMS content management system. A CMS provides the basic framework for your website and allows you to add and edit your products, accept payments and manage your online store. Some examples of these include Shopify, Magento, and big commerce, just to name a few. Beginners often start here before building their own website. Factors to keep in mind when choosing your CMS platform our pricing, scalability, flexibility, and ease of use. Keep in mind that your website or CMS platform acts as your physical shop. This is where people come to interact with you and purchase your goods. This is where you influence them. This is where you impact how likely they are to convert from visitors to customers, and hopefully, repeat customers. So, the decision of where you will be selling your goods is one of the most important ones that you will make. Choose wisely.

The next thing to think about is how you transact with customers. This is a really important decision. Your payment provider is someone that needs to be credible and trustworthy; after all, they're the ones handling your income. Important points to keep in mind here include, compatibility with your e-commerce platform, availability in the countries that your business is targeting, the ability to accept payments in different currencies, the fees charged, reliability and reporting, and usability and customer support. Some payment processes that we highly recommend are Stripe and PayPal.

Lastly, you'll need a good marketing strategy to attract your customers. Let's face it, if you don't attract customers to your online store, you aren't going to make sales. It's not like having a physical storefront where people may just stumble upon you. You have to bring your customers to your online store, and this area will need a good amount of work if you're going to be successful. It's also an area that constantly needs to be revisited, reviewed and adjusted based on what's bringing your traffic at a particular time and what is not. There are a few areas of focus for this one; for example, social media, which has become a channel of Digital Influence and a brilliant tool for building brand awareness. It's almost impossible for new brands to be successful online without some sort of social media presence. Facebook, Twitter, Pinterest, Instagram and other platforms can be used for almost everything, from specific targeting and real time engagement to customer service and direct sales. It's a no-brainer to stay heavily active on these platforms. And the best part of this is, they're free.

Another online tool to consider is SEO, which stands for Search Engine Optimization. This is a technique that helps your business rank higher in search engine results pages. It makes your website more visible to people who are looking for solutions that your product or service can provide. Think about how often you click on page two or three of a Google search to find what you're looking for — hardly ever. So, we don't want our websites to be ranked there, because no one will ever find us. The first page is where you want to be — or want to at least aim to be.

Number three, email marketing. Don't underestimate the power of emails. That is a highly successful tool to keep your audience engaged. You will however need to find a balance between keeping your audience educated and informed, and overwhelming them with too many emails. Start working on building your email list from the beginning. There are some great affordable tools out there that can help you. They help you manage the list of your email contacts and segment your email list. They allow you to customize emails, create, save, edit and manage multiple email templates, as well as get detailed reports on the effectiveness of each campaign. We have the same recommendations that we have for email marketing on MailChimp and Klayviyo. E-commerce is a big playground of its own, because it's a playground that anyone can play on. Yes, there always be bigger, older kids playing there too, but when did that stop the younger kids from playing? Don't be too intimidated, as young kids grow into big kids. They grow and learn along the way. If you want to play on the playground, go for it. I started my e-commerce business from prison. www slickchiselfit.com

So, let's say you've been thinking about opening up your own online business but you don't know where to start, you don't know what you should sell, you don't have any money to invest in products and looking around, and you don't have any room for inventory. Well, that's where drop shipping comes in. With drop shipping, you can sell stuff online without the products ever being in your hand. All you need is a computer, an online store and a basic understanding of how to market and sell online. Here's how it works.

First, you find what you want to sell from a supplier and then list that product on your website at a price you set. Next, when someone places an order on that product, your customer pays you the retail price you've set, and you make a profit. Then you place the order with your supplier at wholesale price and have it shipped directly to your customer. So, let's say you found a bracelet on a supplier's website for $10. You would then list it on your own website for $30, and when the order comes through your website, he would then place your order with your supplier using your customers information, keeping the $20 profit and having that product shipped directly to your customer. That's it. Now, I know you're thinking, why wouldn't somebody just order the bracelet directly from the supplier's website? Well, there's a couple of reasons. First, it's a very big internet, and customers may not know about the supplier to buy from them directly. Second, when people buy things, they're not just buying the products, they're buying into the marketing, positioning, trust, brand and lifestyle. These products represent drop shipping. What you have to focus on is, marketing your products, saying the right things at the right time and providing real value to the right people because you're not warehousing any inventory or dealing with most of the other challenges that come with running an e-commerce business.

You can dropship completely on your own, but be prepared to spend a lot of time researching and negotiating with suppliers to guarantee customer satisfaction. So why do people get into drop shipping? First off, it's really fast and it's super easy to get started. You can dropship with incredibly low investment costs. You also don't need to have an established business entity, when you get started; although i"s probably smart to have one once you start to grow. You don't have to worry about managing inventory, packing or tracking; this means that you can focus almost exclusively on marketing, promotion and merchandise. You have access to millions of products that suppliers are constantly researching to determine what's trending and what will sell. You set the retail price, so you control the margins. Drop shipping is really easy to scale because you can hire virtual assistants as order volume increases.

Of course, there are some challenges associated with drop shipping. First off, because it's really easy to get started, there's a really high potential for competition. That's why I recommend you start off with finding a niche audience, like dog lovers or gamers, so you can operate with less competition. Next, there are supplier errors; although this is uncommon, it is inevitable that a supplier will mistakenly ship the wrong product to your customer. If this happens, don't take it personally. Instead, handle the return like a professional; either order a brand-new product from the supplier, or offer a full refund. Also, since many drop shipping suppliers are based in China, shipping times are generally longer, and this can turn some customers off. The solution to this is ePacket, which makes it easier, delivering some orders in as little as two weeks. But generally speaking, if you make your shipping window clear throughout the buying process, many visitors will appreciate it, especially if you're selling an item in a niche where delivery times are a little less crucial.

Once you have all that, you need to create a plan for sending traffic to your store. It is important to try to produce quality content for your store. Eye-catching product photos that will make great posts for your blog, enough for your audience to engage are important. This will make your audience want to know more about your products, how they can be used, and the story behind them.

Now that we've covered all the things you need to get started, here are a few additional things to keep in mind. One, drop shipping is pretty easy to learn, but there is still a learning curve, and you will certainly experience challenges along the way. However, these challenges or mistakes can become learning opportunities. Also, if you can develop resilience along the way, there are plenty of people out there who are successful in drop shipping products too. Second, while there is a significant advantage in terms of capital investment over traditional e-commerce, drop shipping isn't free. You'll likely have to spend money to drive traffic and market your products. Three, there is no overnight success in this; it is not a get-rich-quick scheme. Drop shipping still requires you to work consistently for your store. Truly, you will need to dedicate less time compared to a traditional e-commerce business, but then again, it is not going to succeed without your hard work. You will always need to invest time to improve your business.

Another important thing to note is, don't source copyright items. This is illegal. The aim here is to run a legit business. You can always add more inventory as you become comfortable, but it's better to start small and build than it is to start big and become overwhelmed. When you get to the point where you feel comfortable with drop shipping, diversify. Many drop shippers don't rely on a single store for their entire income stream, but operate a series of stores and target various niches to build multiple sources of income.

EPILOGUE

Even though I was doing time, I didn't have time. I was busy preparing myself to break the generational curse that had been upon my community for a long time. For the most part, in my community, we were either working a job for a living or going to prison, with no legal wealth or knowledge being passed along to the next generation; no proper knowledge of self, our potential, and how to take care of our health, both mentally and physically. We need to know that the more we know as a community, the more we'll grow as a community. And the knowledge needs to come from diverse sources because although we're one and the same, everyone can't relate.

To wrap things up, I'm going to paraphrase a word eloquently spoken by Karim Ellis. Let me ask you something, when it comes to your time or how you spend it, are you playing chess or checkers? When it comes to your life and your goals, dreams and aspirations, are you playing checkers? Or are you playing chess? In the game of checkers, your job is to take all your game pieces and try to wipe out the opposing player's pieces; just jump over game pieces until you wipe everything out. Whereas, in the game of chess, I'm taking all my game pieces, and I'm focused on putting one piece in checkmate. That's the king. That means every piece I have under my control will focus on one thing; I'm not trying to wipe out the whole board, I'm simply trying to wipe out that one piece of the puzzle. The game of chess and checkers is played on an identical board, so you have to be intentionally aware of what game you're playing. If you spend your time playing checkers. That means you're not going to get anything worthwhile accomplished, as you're not focused on one thing. You're easily thrown off your pivot by whatever piece comes in front of you, regardless of its significance. But for the folks who play chess, they got it figured out; you're not trying to jump over everything that's laying in front of you. You understand that it's okay to let people pass you, it's okay to sacrifice relationships, and it's okay to walk away from jobs in order to give yourself better positioning. All of these moves are dependent on how they align with the pursuit of your goals and your dreams. That's the difference between checkers and chess. See, when I play chess with my life and with my time, that means I'm strategic in my approach. I'm taking all my gifts, all my talents, my effort, my energy, my education. That means I'm focused on learning the right things — not just everything. My inner circle are the folks I can network with and connect my net worth with. Everything is geared toward the pursuit of my goal because at the end of my life, I want to say "check mate." Life is a game of chess, so if you're playing checkers, you automatically lose.

GLOSSARY OF TERMS

ALEC - The American Legislative Exchange Council (ALEC) is a nonprofit organization of conservative state legislators and private sector representatives who draft and share model legislation for distribution among state governments in the United States. ALEC provides a forum for state legislators and private sector members to collaborate on model bills—draft legislation that members may customize and introduce for debate in their own state legislatures.

Bond - A bond is a fixed-income instrument that represents a loan made by an investor to a borrower (typically corporate or governmental). A bond could be thought of as an I.O.U. between the lender and borrower that includes the details of the loan and its payments. Bonds are used by companies, municipalities, states, and sovereign governments to finance projects and operations. Owners of bonds are debtholders, or creditors, of the issuer. Bond details include the end date when the principal of the loan is due to be paid to the bond owner and usually include the terms for variable or fixed interest payments made by the borrower.

Commodity - , a commodity is an economic good, usually a resource, that has full or substantial fungibility: that is, the market treats instances of the good as equivalent or nearly so with no regard to who produced them. Most commodities are raw materials, basic resources, agricultural, or mining products, such as iron ore, sugar, or grains like rice and wheat.

Contraband - goods that have been imported or exported illegally.

Futures – a futures contract (sometimes called a futures) is a standardized legal contract to buy or sell something at a predetermined price for delivery at a specified time in the future, between parties not yet known to each other. The asset transacted is usually a commodity or financial instrument.

Hedge Fund -A hedge fund is a pooled investment fund that trades in relatively liquid assets and is able to make extensive use of more complex trading, portfolio-construction, and risk management techniques in an attempt to improve performance, such as short selling, leverage, and derivatives.

ICO- An initial coin offering (ICO) is the cryptocurrency industry's equivalent to an initial public offering (IPO). A company seeking to raise money to create a new coin, app, or service can launch an ICO as a way to raise funds. Interested investors can buy into an initial coin offering to receive a new cryptocurrency token issued by the company. This token may have some utility related to the product or service that the company is offering, or it may just represent a stake in the company or project.

IMF- The International Monetary Fund (IMF) is an international organization that promotes global economic growth and financial stability, encourages international trade, and reduces poverty.

IPO- An initial public offering (IPO) or stock launch is a public offering in which shares of a company are sold to institutional investors and usually also to retail (individual) investors. An IPO is typically underwritten by one or more investment banks, who also arrange for the shares to be listed on one or more stock exchanges. Through this process, colloquially known as floating, or going public, a privately held company is transformed into a public company. Initial public offerings can be used to raise new equity capital for companies, to monetize the investments of private shareholders such as company founders or private equity investors, and to enable easy trading of existing holdings or future capital raising by becoming publicly traded.

KYC-The know your customer or know your client (KYC) guidelines in financial services require that professionals make an effort to verify the identity, suitability, and risks involved with maintaining a business relationship.

OPM- other people's money, or OPM, is a slang term that refers to financial leverage. Other people's money refers to borrowed capital that is used to increase the potential returns as well as the risks of an investment. OPM can be used by individuals or by corporations.

P2P- Peer-to-peer (P2P) is a decentralized communications model in which each party has the same capabilities and either party can initiate a communication session.

Securities market- Security market is a component of the wider financial market where securities can be bought and sold between subjects of the economy, on the basis of demand and supply. Security markets encompasses stock markets, bond markets and derivatives markets where prices can be determined and participants both professional and non professional can meet.

Stable coin- Stablecoins are cryptocurrencies where the price is designed to be pegged to a cryptocurrency, fiat money, or to exchange-traded commodities (such as precious metals or industrial metals).

ABOUT AUTHOR

Malik ibn Lerow, published model, actor, entrepreneur, and trader who served over a decade behind bars in the Georgia penal system. He is the founder of brands Slick Chisel Fitness and Chisel'd Supplements. These brands encourage active living and healthy nutrition to combat obesity and heart disease. He is dubbed Alpha Convict because of his strong example for at risk youth and the millions of people under correctional supervision nationwide. You can see more of Malik on Instagram @alphacon_model

www.ingramcontent.com/pod-product-compliance
Lightning Source LLC
Chambersburg PA
CBHW072156090426
42740CB00012B/2288
9780578375243